MASTER
STORYTELLER

MASTER
STORYTELLER

GOD'S ORAL COMMUNICATION IN THE BIBLE AND HEBREW TRADITION

BY

DAVID SWARR, PHD.

RICKI GIDOOMAL

PSALM ARAUJO

CENTER FOR ORAL SCRIPTURES

master-storyteller.net

Master Storyteller Copyright © David Swarr, Ricki Gidoomal, Psalm Araujo, 2017

Limited Edition

ISBN: 978-1-9791960-6-2

Published by The Center for Oral Scriptures
in conjunction with The Lausanne Movement
www.4220foundation.com
www.lausanne.org
PO BOX 23023
Richmond
VA, 23223
USA
info@4220foundation.com
--

Endorsements

I<small>N THIS THOUGHT-PROVOKING</small> book and the evocative short films that accompany it, Swarr, Gidoomal and Araujo convincingly present God as the master of oral communication. He spoke creation into being, revealed himself through symbol, ritual and celebration, and delights in the vast array of artistic expressions extending his kingdom around the world. The authors have also created an outstanding online learning platform that connects the principles of the book to a wide array of digital resources for further exploration and discovery. Together, this compendium of resources equips and inspires us to follow the eternal storyteller's example in drawing from a range of artistic forms when communicating his story within our own communities and beyond.

Robin P. Harris, PhD., Director of Center for Excellence in World Arts at GIAL, President of International Council of Ethnodoxologists

Without a doubt, this is the first book that presents a solid case for orality from the perspective of the whole Bible. It begins by identifying God as the Master Storyteller, continuing with the history of mankind and redemption in Christ and culminating with an invitation for everyone to enter in and participate in God's story. As you read through this book, you can prayerfully pause and reflect at the different layers of spiritual depth, and see how you are challenged to respond. The visual and aural interjections embedded in this book intensify an understanding of orality which consequently inspires innovative strategies for the Great

Commission. The Master Storyteller is a succinct biblical theology of orality. This is a highly recommended book and I am certain that it will be a breath of life that can invigorate every pastor, educator, theologian, missionary and believer as they fulfill the story of their lives in His Story.

Rev. Romerlito C. Macalinao, Ed.D., President/CEO of
Wycliffe Bible Translators Philippines, Inc.

God as the 'Master Storyteller' comes at a kairos time with great opportunity for the global church in advancing the Gospel across all cultures. Matthew's account of the Great Commission has both a geo-ethnic and a generational implication for mission. In the power and presence of Christ, the church has a mandate to make disciples of 'all nations' and 'to the very end of the age'. This double perspective must shape our missional approach as we partner, pray and plan in 'teaching disciples to obey all the commands Jesus has given. God's Word as the Great Story uniquely communicates to us in all languages, across all cultures and in all generations. I hope this book, with its engaging style and substance will challenge and release the creativity of a new generation of reflective mission practitioners to respond to the timely Cape Town Commitment call of "eradication of Bible poverty in the world and Bible ignorance in the church". Here is a rich treasure for leaders, gatekeepers, and decision makers in the global church.

Nana Yaw Offei Awuku, Director of Younger Leaders Generation (YLGen)
The Lausanne Movement

Foreword

I SAT SPELL-BOUND watching the premier of the 'Master Storyteller'—three short films that artfully visualize how our God communicates orally. The occasion of this premier was the Lausanne Younger Leaders Generation (YLGen) meeting in Jakarta, Indonesia. The setting was a beautiful Christian university campus, and in this workshop I was amongst younger leaders from around the world. I realized this was a watershed moment for the journey of orality and the next generation.

Earlier this century, the Lausanne Movement facilitated the birthing of 'orality' through the creation of the International Orality Network. The issue of making disciples of oral learners gained focused attention and changed trajectories for many organizations around the world. Many people in the non-West felt they were understood for the first time. People said to me repeatedly, 'our country, and indeed, our continent is all oral, and now we feel empowered to minister in the way we normally do it in our culture.'

Sitting in the audience with the next generation of younger leaders and watching the films reminded me of Deuteronomy 31:19 and Revelation 15:3. Moses was instructed to write down a song and teach it to the children of Israel; this same song is sung in Revelation 15:3. This is incredible! What was recorded in oral form from God onto tablets of stone is repeated generation after generation by memory, so that ultimately on that day, as portrayed in the book of Revelation, it is sung back to God. Imagine the voice of God recorded into the many mediums, one day reverberating back to God by a chorus of voices. There is something about God's primary means of communication—orality—that is very special. He speaks tenderly in whispers and boldly in shouts.

The new generation of leaders in this century are becoming unshackled from textual literacy and are participating in communication that is more oral and visual. How will they be unleashed? How will they bring the Gospel to a world which hungers for truth? What means will they have to build momentum?

Coauthors Dr. Swarr, Gidoomal and Araujo, have over half a century of collective experience in Israel. Each one in their own right can provide meaningful books; however, they choose to collaborate in a relational way so as to model how oral learners work. This book is a unique telling of God's demonstrative words, work and symbols.

The book you hold is also part of a media ecosystem that includes film, digital art, audio, print and social media. This interactive ecosystem encourages the unleashing of creativity and invites communal conversations about God's heart for the nations. Through the films, Araujo and Gidoomal bring God's creativity, symbols and rituals alive! These assist us in exploring and discovering our creative God, and the creativity within us.

This is an ambitious project, but one that aims to speak to multiple generations about God and how a new generation can be unleashed for the Kingdom. You will go deeper in your understanding of God, you will see new ways of discipleship, and you will be changed by the multifaceted approach of telling God's creative Word!

May I commend this book to you.

Samuel E. Chiang
Lausanne Catalyst—Orality
President and CEO
Seed Company

Contents

Preface

THE PURPOSE OF this book is to inspire leaders, gatekeepers and decision makers in the global church to think outside the box about the creative possibilities God gives us to communicate his Word orally. We especially want to stimulate the innovative energies of young people to use their gifts of oral communication to mirror the beautiful and diverse ways that God communicates with us. We don't want Christians to feel limited by a cultural dependence on text when communicating who God is to others. Fully recognizing the power and authority of God's Word throughout history, we want the Church to be liberated to see the God of the Bible as the greatest communicator of all, the Master Storyteller, and to conduct ourselves accordingly.

The chapters are organized around three main themes:

1) God as an oral communicator
2) His demonstration of a multiplicity of oral communication methods and the power they have to shape identities, families, communities and cultures
3) Ways in which followers of Jesus can tap into God's incredible creativity and vast array of oral tools to effect change and improve lives in their own settings

Specifically, the introduction challenges us to consider why we need to focus on oral communication and not just text. Chapter one explores how God is an oral communicator through his living Word. Chapters two through eight illustrate the range of oral methods and media God uses to communicate his relationship with us throughout Scripture. Chapter nine is a call to use these methods God has given us and to create with God, as his story is enacted through us. The epilogue then addresses critical issues to make it possible for all oral learners to engage with God's Word.

Master Storyteller is more than a printed book. Each of the three themes of the book is accompanied by a short film. Links to these films are embedded in the text and are an integral part of the content. For best understanding and presentation, it is intended that each film be initially viewed only at the point the reader comes across it within the body of the book. Further, an interactive digital learning platform has been designed to facilitate personal and communal growth. Discussion questions, additional resources, and eventually further audio and video components will enable a growing dialogue.

A team has contributed to the writing of this book as well as the accompanying short film productions and digital media platform.

David Swarr serves as Executive Director of International Orality Network (ION) and is President and CEO of 4.2.20 Foundation. He previously served on the leadership team of ION and stewarded the Audio Scripture Engagement portfolio. David was also a founder, President and CEO of Davar Partners International, an audio Scripture engagement organization with over 600 partner organizations in 90 nations. David grew up in the Middle East and speaks fluent Hebrew. He has a rich background in cross cultural leadership and holds a PhD in intercultural organizational leadership. Currently, David and his wife split their time between Israel and the United States.

Ricki Gidoomal serves as Chief of Staff of 4.2.20 Foundation and as Senior Associate of Communications for the International Orality Network. He produced the Master Storyteller film trilogy that accompanies this content. He holds an MA in Russian & Linguistics from the University of Oxford, with specialization in Ancient Dialect and Second Language Acquisition. Ricki also facilitates the Lausanne Younger Leaders

Generation (YLGen) Orality Interest Group and serves on the Lausanne Technology Issues Network. Ricki grew up in the United Kingdom and currently lives in Israel with his family.

Psalm Araujo works as Creative Director of Communications and Special Projects of 4.2.20 Foundation. She directed the Master Storyteller short film trilogy, all filmed in Israel. She holds a degree in Interdisciplinary Studies from Wheaton College, combining Film, Media, Communication & Culture, with additional studies at Hebrew University. She has experience in music, acting and directing both in theatre and film in Hong Kong, Israel, and the United Kingdom. She is also a singer song-writer with two albums, *Story* and *Waking up the Storm*. Psalm grew up between Israel and Richmond, Virginia, and currently travels between the two with her husband.

While we represent different backgrounds, what we share in common is extensive exposure to the land of the Bible and to Hebrew language and tradition. This has been the seedbed out of which this production has grown. Some of the chapters are written predominantly by one author while other chapters have contributions from all three. We would also like to thank Sharon Swarr, Arielle Swarr, Joni Chiang, Stan Horst, and Mary Katherine Stender for their excellent editorial and proofing work. Thanks also to Joni Chiang for creating the graphics.

We have not attempted to make this a comprehensive biblical or historical study. Rather, our purpose is to open windows through which to view God as the master oral communicator who sets the example for what we too can do under the creative direction of the Holy Spirit. Our hope is that as you apply the principles in this book you will add your stories to the conversation. We hope you find this book useful to yourself and your communities as a source of inspiration and discipleship.

David Swarr
Ricki Gidoomal
Psalm Araujo

Introduction

Oral communication

*Orality definition: a reliance on spoken, rather than written,
language for communication.*

WE ARE ALL oral learners. We didn't lie in our mother's arms learning our first words from the dictionary. Oral communicators are those whose primary way of learning and passing on information is through visual, aural, or sensory means as opposed to text. From Moses to Aristotle to Einstein, we all learned our mother tongue orally.

In the literate world we have historically thought of orality and textuality in a dichotomized manner. We separate the population into two groups: the literate and illiterate. However, scholars have recently come to understand orality more accurately as reflected in a continuum. We are all oral learners, but some of us are also textual learners. Dr. Grant Lovejoy, Director of Orality Strategies for the International Mission Board, writes in his article "The Extent of Orality" that approximately 80 percent of the world prefer to learn orally.[1]

Since God created us as oral learners he uses oral ways to communicate with us. This may seem like an obvious observation, and yet the way

---

1 Grant Lovejoy, "The Extent of Orality: 2012 Update," *Orality Journal* 1, No. 1 (2012).

most Christians communicate God's Word relies foremost on a culture of dependence on written text—words on a page. But God's Word is bigger than the constrictions of text. God chose an oral communication master plan through which anyone anywhere could know him.

Why was Scripture in text necessary?

In Romans 1:20, the Apostle Paul writes, *"For since the creation of the world God's invisible qualities—his eternal power and divine nature—have been clearly seen, being understood from what has been made, so that people are without excuse."*[2] If through the evidence of nature alone God judges mankind to be without excuse in relation to him, what then is the necessity of the written record we call the Bible?

Well, it turns out that human beings are finite and our capacity to learn and remember is limited. So God gave us the written word for the multiplication of knowledge as one of a wide array of communication gifts. The prophet Daniel foretold that in the latter days knowledge would abound and increase on the earth.[3] Text increases our ability to store and retrieve information across time and space. No longer must a person be present in order to tell the story to others. It also expands our ability to communicate across linguistic and cultural barriers, by making the message replicable and transferable.

However, perhaps the greatest contribution of text is that it supplied a means for God to give us an authoritative record, the final authority for life and practice. When a story is conveyed verbally, where does the authenticating authority lie? Is it with the storyteller? What is to prevent the story from being changed in the telling from one person to another, or from one culture to another? The written Bible is God's solution to this problem. In this way, what began as the story of freedom and salvation for one people in the Bible can become the story for all people today.

---

2   Rom 1:20 NIV

3   Dn 12:4

But the story doesn't end with the text. Media theorist Marshall McLuhan wrote, "The medium is the message"[4]—meaning the medium we use to communicate is also what we are communicating. Too often we communicate using a medium that does not allow people to learn and relate to the power of God's Word, alive and active in the world, not just stagnant on a page.

Beyond text

While we must appreciate the importance and necessity of the written record, Hebrews 4:12 reminds us that *"the word of God is living and active."*[5] As will be discussed later, *davar* is Hebrew for "word" and is used to refer both to the Incarnate Word, Jesus, and to the Scriptures. The Davar—The Word—is an extension and manifestation of the person of Jesus. The Word of God is a deposit of the very being of the God of the universe—a repository of his person, bearing his likeness and reflecting his glory. It is alive and active, creative and powerful.

In this way the words "Bible" and "Scripture," which both refer to a written text, are inadequate to represent the Word of God, for they merely indicate its packaging. The Word of God was before and will be after script and the printed or digital text, for it is the living essence which is in, and which speaks and creates through, what we read or hear. God's Word speaks every language, in every time, to all humanity.

Full circle

It can be argued that humanity has come full circle in our communication methods—from oral to written text to oral again. What started as pictures on a rock or wall developed into visual symbols written on the ground, on scrolls, tablets and then books. We are now at the close of an era which Professor Thomas Pettitt of the University of Southern Denmark

---

4 Marshall McLuhan, *Understanding Media: The Extensions of Man* (New York: McGraw Hill 1964).
5 Heb 4:12 ESV

refers to as the "Gutenberg Parenthesis."[6] Gutenberg's printing press made textual content readily accessible to the masses and brought about a revolution in learning. Text has given us extremely valuable tools, but it has not changed the basic nature of humankind as oral learners. And with today's technologies, even the textually dependent world is moving beyond using text alone. While human history began with oral communication and added textual communication technologies along the way, it is now coming full circle—at a much higher level in which even technology is no longer print dependent.

This sequence in the development of how knowledge is conveyed has implications for educational systems in all fields. If indeed orality is the broader context into which textuality fits as a component, then we must rethink our approach to education in the context of academic institutions, churches, the workplace or missions. In fact, it will force us to rethink and change our language about learning and education. Perceptions of whether an individual is more or less "educated" have commonly been based upon assumptions that relate education to textuality. But learning is about to take a quantum leap forward—one in which text is but one component of a broader learning environment.

For theological education and leadership development this issue bears heavy consideration. Christian educators and practitioners alike must determine whether they will be the forerunners and innovators of this movement or run the risk of being left behind.

6 Tom Pettitt, "Before the Gutenberg Parenthesis: Elizabethan-American Compatibilities," *academia.edu*, accessed Aug. 25, 2017, http://www.academia.edu/2946207/Before_the_Gutenberg_Parenthesis_Elizabethan-American_Compatibilities.

Chapter 1

God Communicates Out Loud

To Him who rides upon the highest heavens, which are from ancient times;
Behold, He speaks forth His voice, a mighty voice.

– Psalm 68:33 NASB

Empowered words

Too often when we think about God, we tame him to the pages of a book, sitting quietly on our shelf. But the maker of the universe cannot be controlled and will not remain silent. Genesis 1, the opening of the Bible leads with, *"In the beginning God created the heavens and the earth...and God said, 'let there be light', and there was light...."*[7] God speaks and creates; in fact, he creates by speaking. God speaks and the heavens and earth are created. The very first thing God reveals about himself is that he is both a creator and a communicator, and the rest of the chapter highlights this with the repeated phrase *"and God said..."* The second place in the Bible that starts similarly is John 1:1—*"In the beginning was the Word..."*[8] Just like Genesis, John tells us that God is creator and communicator, with a special emphasis on his character as a communicator. The Word was with God, the Word was God and everything created was created through the Word.

In order to fully grasp the power of the meaning of *The Word*, it's important to take a step back and understand the meaning of the language used to describe this passage. What we refer to as The Gospel of John may have been recorded in Greek, but as an oral learner from Galilee whose mother tongue was not Greek, John's thought process would have been Aramaic. His biblical understanding would have come from the Old Testament (Hebrew Bible), so although the early records use the Greek *logos* John would have been thinking the Hebrew *davar*, the word used in the Old Testament. In his mother tongue, John would have said to his contemporaries, *"In the beginning was the davar,"* which is translated into English as *"in the beginning was the word."* But this translation is too simplistic.

Davar cannot be translated merely as "word" because it means so much more. While English also uses "word" to translate the Greek words *logos* and *rhema* that are used in the New Testament, the Hebrew davar encompasses and surpasses the meanings of both *logos* and *rhema*. It can mean word, utterance, prophetic message, purpose, cause, power, matter, an object or even a text. It can be written, spoken, visual or experienced.

---

7 Gn 1:1,3 ESV
8 Jn 1:1 ESV

Davar occurs over 1400 times in Scripture and is translated by 85 different English words in the King James Version. Its root verb occurs over 1100 times and requires 45 different English words. In Hebrew, "nothing" is *shume-dabar*—literally "no-thing." "No matter" is *ein-dabar*, or the absence of davar. *Le-daber* is translated "to speak" or "to utter," but *le-daber* is so much more than what we think of as speaking. It is both the utterance itself and simultaneously its creative act: *"and God said, 'let there be light,' and there was light."*[9] Davar is both the "word" and the accompanying power to fulfill what is uttered.

Several passages underscore this truth. Colossians 1:15-17 refers to Jesus as the incarnate Word: *"He is the image of the invisible God, the firstborn of all creation. For by him all things were created, in heaven and on earth, visible and invisible... all things were created through him and for him. And he is before all things, and in him all things hold together."*[10] In Isaiah 55:11 the word (davar) goes out of God's mouth to accomplish a task. This passage states that the davar never returns void; it always achieves its purpose. It has the power of life and gives life to those that hear it. In modern Hebrew, *Dvar Adonai*, the "Word of God" is used to refer both to the Bible and to the incarnate Word, Jesus. The apostle John was clearly referring to a person. Jesus also referred to himself as the living Word. 1 John 1:1 refers to the "Word of life" or the "living Word."

What does this tell us? The Davar is first and foremost a person, then an utterance bearing the creative power of the person, which brings into being some "thing" tangible in our world. The process can be described as follows: The Word (Davar), utters a word (medaber), which creates a thing (davar). The resulting creation is an extension and manifestation of its creator.

---

9 Gn 1:3 ESV
10 Col 1:15-17 ESV

THE WORD
"DAVAR"

UTTERS A WORD

"MEDABER"

WHICH CREATES A THING

"DAVAR"

THE RESULTING CREATION IS AN EXTENSION
AND MANIFESTATION OF ITS CREATOR

MAN

Through the understanding of this language we can see that God is oral; his very being is expressed in his davar (word). Creation, which came into being and is sustained by the Word, is an extension of his person and is therefore also oral. As a result, humankind, created in the image of God, is also innately oral in being.

"Let there be light"—no other words have so shaped the course of history and destiny of humanity except perhaps one other sentence spoken in a darkened garden: *"Father, your will be done."*[11] These words too, though spoken much later in history, underpin the very foundations of our universe and hold together our existence.

Power beyond words

The quantity of God's oral communication, his very voice, far surpasses anything written, and the Bible is a condensed record of God's oral communication. Scripture tells us this in John 21:25, which states that the whole world could not contain the books written about all that Jesus said

---

11 Gn 1:3; Mt 26:42 ESV

4

and did. God whispered to Elijah, spoke in a still, small voice to Moses and called to Samuel in the night. His voice was heard again and again. Whether this was a voice they heard with their ears or just in their minds is not always clear from the context, but we can be sure that it was not just textual. God's Davar has been going forth since the beginning of time and continues unabated to this day.

Even without words God whispers and shouts. His Word tells us that he spoke through angels, through dreams and visions, through prophets and even a donkey. He communicated through miracles and dramatic interventions in nature. God speaks through all of creation, natural and spiritual. In the next chapters, let's look at a few of the examples in Scripture in which God goes beyond language to amplify his voice.

Reflection Questions

1) What is the significance of "word" (*davar*) as distinct from the word "Bible"?

2) What does this distinction tell us about creation?

3) Can you recall an experience of how God has communicated to you or your community, beyond the written text of Scripture?

Chapter 2

The Greatest Show in the Universe

For since the creation of the world God's invisible qualities—
his eternal power and divine nature—have been clearly seen,
being understood from what has been made, so that people are
without excuse.

– Romans 1:20 NIV

God speaks through nature

You and I are witnesses to the greatest show in the universe, one that encompasses all of our senses. This production has been playing constantly since the dawn of time. It is the only show experienced by every human being who has ever lived—regardless of age, gender, race, language, education, socioeconomic status or geographic location. Indeed, the Creator of the universe is a god of media! He has given us senses so we might experience the wonder of who he is. The "media production" we call the universe is full of God on display. He is the producer, the director and the central character of the greatest show of all time.

God did not simply create the universe to then abandon it. Far from it! God's voice sounds through every aspect of creation, from the singing of the birds to the crashing waves of the sea. The endless stars and galaxies speak of his infinite greatness, while the atomic world tells of his minute attention to detail. The diversity of colors and tastes speak of his creativity and of his love. He uses every means possible to communicate to human beings who he is and the way for us to prosper in every dimension of life. In this chapter, we will explore how God uses the specific symbol of the garden to communicate orally, using all the senses, who he is in relation to his creation.

Talking gardens

Just as every song, painting, poem or novel is both a self-revelation and message from its maker, the same can be said of gardens and their designers. Some are simple; others are complex and intricate. Some are very ordered, manicured and symmetrical; others are more wild or natural. Whether the royal gardens in London, the hanging gardens of ancient Persia, or even a "secret garden" written about in literature, each is an expression of the personality, imagination, values and preferences of its designer.

In Genesis we learn of a great garden. The gardener was God himself and he called it Eden, or Paradise. God took meticulous care in creating the garden and placed in it all forms of life—not only plant life but animals, fish and fowl. And it was beautiful with lush arrays of color, scintillating sounds, smells and textures beyond measure, each unique and varied. It was teeming with life. The entire ecosystem was life-giving and sustaining. While immensely diverse it was, at the same time, ordered and balanced. It was harmonious with no hint of death or destruction. It was simultaneously a place of power and of peace. Through this garden God communicated his passion for beauty, his endless creativity, his care for order as well as diversity, and so much more.

Around the world there are marvels of human ingenuity expressed through architecture, from the pyramids and ancient Mayan temples, to the modern towers of Hong Kong, New York and Dubai. But none of these begin to rival the creative majesty of the Garden of Eden. All, at best, are a dim reflection of a very small portion of the ever-changing masterpiece of God's creation, which we have the privilege of experiencing through our senses. Humanity's artistic creations are static, with limits of space and time. One can return and see the same human-made painting, sculpture and building, or listen to the same song again—but God's creative genius is limitless and cannot be bound to time and space. No snowflake or human ear is the same as any other. Every sunset changes uniquely before our eyes. The chorus of birds at sunrise is never repeated exactly, nor the patterns of the waves or clouds.

Beyond displaying God's unrivaled beauty in design, the Garden of Eden also communicated God's love for humankind because it was for Adam and Eve to enjoy. They were to enjoy the fruit, the living creatures, the environment and one another. He designed it as a place of meeting and intimacy. It was conducive to fellowship—a place for communication between God and humankind as they delight in one another.

Further, God communicated the value he has for humankind, his plan and calling, by giving them authority over it. The Garden was the first school, way ahead of today's systems and theories of learning! God's method of instruction might be what is referred to in educational circles today as the "total physical response" approach—it involved all the senses. Adam and Eve learned by observation, participation and application. He gave them the role of naming the animals, allowing them to take part in the creative process. But God did not leave them to learn solely on their own. Daily he came and modeled the way to relate among themselves and to care for creation. Just as in any culture's socialization process today, in the Garden, values were caught as much as taught. By placing in the Garden a tree from which he forbade them to eat, God revealed his commitment to freedom of choice. He also demonstrated his own dedication to truth through the consequences he gave. God revealed that his desire is for humans to grow in knowledge and understanding—to explore and learn from his creation.

To conclude, the foundational instruction to the parents of humankind was entirely oral. It was conducted in the context and for the purpose of relationship. Relationships are to be experienced. They are not predominantly a textual exchange. Rather, intimate communication is primarily oral. Through the Garden and all of creation God is communicating his desire for relationship with us. And even today, all of creation is singing to us about this relationship. Nature displays the glory of God and yet also tells the story of a broken relationship between God and humanity. Though the earth currently suffers under the fallenness of our stewardship, Scripture speaks to us of the renewal of all creation— and we are a part of that story! The prophets foretold that there will come a time when God's people will experience the trees clapping, hills singing, and the lion and lamb playing together.

"In the Beginning" is a short film set in the Garden of Eden and told in the form of a poem from the perspective of Adam and Eve. The story highlights how God shows his character in the world and nature and demonstrates relationship. Even beyond the scope of the garden, creation continues to speak. Watch here:

https://master-storyteller.net/films/in-the-beginning

Reflection Questions

1) How does the way God designed the Garden of Eden reflect his character and values?

2) How does nature tell of a broken relationship today, and how can we help restore this relationship?

3) What are some ways that we can be more responsive to God's communication to us through nature?

Chapter 3

God's Strategy for an Oral Nation

Hear, O Israel: The Lord our God, the Lord is one. You shall love the Lord your God with all your heart and with all your soul and with all your might. And these words that I command you today shall be on your heart. You shall teach them diligently to your children, and shall talk of them when you sit in your house, and when you walk by the way, and when you lie down, and when you rise.

– Deuteronomy 6:4-7 ESV

The Sh'ma

Just as God communicates through nature, he also speaks through the oral practices of community. For example, the foundation of God's communication to the Israelites was based upon the relational principles of speaking, listening and hearing with the whole heart and the whole body. This is apparent in the scriptural statement known as the *Sh'ma*, the Hebrew word that means "hear" named after the passage in Deuteronomy 6. Jesus said this was the most important of all commandments. God commands us to hear him, to love him with everything in us, and to embody his words in every aspect of our lives, from generation to generation.

In our modern text-based culture, we rarely discuss the practices of ancient Israel as an oral people. We discuss the stories of the Bible, but rarely the methods of communication God used in and through his people over time. Understanding these methods can open up a much larger perspective into the immense character of God. Further, when we grasp these patterns of communication that God used to speak to his people, we can mirror these ways for more effective communication of who he is in our communities today.

In this chapter we will see that throughout the Old Testament God had an intentional and comprehensive strategy for instructing his oral nation, community by community. There are three main ways this strategy worked: individual and family engagement, regular corporate learning events, and strategically dispersed oral learning centers.

Individual and family engagement

The first element of God's strategy began with daily meditation on the oral Word of God. This consisted of personal and family engagement with God's Word that was not textual, but oral. The setting was communal, and "family" included the extended family, unlike western nuclear families today. God's instruction, first given through Moses, was to be passed on from one generation to the next within the family. They were to think about it continually, meditating and talking about it during each phase of the day whether sitting at the table, lying on their cots, or walking to the well. The stories were to be shared with their children on the way to the market and discussed with them around the fire at night. Stories were told, songs sung, and principles internalized and memorized.

Regular corporate learning events

The second component of God's strategy for his oral nation was corporate learning. This system of learning was designed around a solar calendar, was event and ritual driven, and it had designated places of worship and meeting.

Calendar

A simple solar-lunar calendar, God's daily and monthly timekeeping system, was unmistakable for all who could see. It was easily learned by children and required no particular educational experience or socioeconomic standing to understand. By using this calendar, God left no room for excuses when it came to participation in regular ritual. Operating on this solar calendar, God instructed Israel on how to establish numerous ceremonies for daily, weekly and monthly practice designed to enhance relationships with God and one another. These ritual practices involved experiential and visual depiction of the requirements for healthy personal and community life. The entire system had little textual input, and where text was used it was shared orally with the public, making it easy for all to understand.

Events and rituals

God invoked times for the community to gather together for corporate celebration and learning. These events drew the nation together to celebrate and commemorate stories of what God had done in their history.

One such ritual was gathering for the public reading of the law of God. Over and over in Scripture, God instructed his people to read his Word out loud in community. The Words of God were never meant to be tucked away on a shelf or only to be heard by scholars. For example, Moses instructed Israel to gather for public reading of the law of God.

Every segment of the community was to be involved. As seen later in the time of Nehemiah, no one *"who could hear with understanding"* was exempt.[12] The purpose was for all to hear, learn, observe and act upon what they had heard. Moses also clearly specified that women, children and even aliens within the community were to participate.[13] This principle of including everyone in corporate worship is a vital part of how God communicates his will and love in community.

Further, the observance of specific festival practices educated the people in understanding sin, judgement and forgiveness, as well as faith and trust in God as provider and deliverer. There were seven annual biblical festivals[14] also called "appointed times" or "holy convocations." Three of them were "pilgrimage" festivals in which the entire nation was to gather to the sacred meeting place. These three festivals were the Feast of Unleavened Bread (Passover/Pesach), the Feast of Weeks (Shavuot) and the Feast of Tabernacles (Sukkot).

In the time of Jesus it was common practice for entire extended families to travel together from their towns and villages to Jerusalem for the festivals; Jesus himself went regularly when he was a child. This was a large-scale community event. The account of one such festival gathering in the time of Nehemiah depicts what would have typically taken place. From a raised platform, the priest read the book of the law to all the people for a quarter of the day (three hours). Then the levitical leaders led in discussion with questions and answers so that all would understand. This pattern continued for the duration of the seven days of the festival. When the people heard and understood the instructions they then put into practice what they had learned. The rest of the story tells of the community action and reformation that took place as a result of the public reading and application of God's Word.[15]

---

12 Neh 8:2
13 Dt 31:11-13
14 Lv 23
15 Neh 8:1-9:3

Place of worship and meeting

The place of worship itself was significant in God's teaching strategy. God specified that the nation should gather to the place that God would choose.[16] Very detailed instructions were given concerning its layout, each of the articles and their placement within the Tabernacle, and later the Temple. Every item, aspect and practice conveyed meaning and instruction. The location of the Temple was also highly symbolic: God's "house"—the place of worship and atonement for the people of Israel—was built upon the mountaintop where Abraham had been called upon to sacrifice his only son. This foreshadowed the eternal sacrifice of God's own son on the same mountain, and the place to which the Messiah will return to establish God's house and rule.

Finally, it was of critical importance to have a reference point of religious authority that the people could point to. The Temple was the place of God's dwelling—the earthly seat of authority. In every system there is always a final authority; it may be a nation's constitution, a monarch or a collective group. When God chose the place for his dwelling, the message was, "I am, and my Word is, the final authority for life and practice."

Strategically dispersed oral learning centers

A third component of God's strategy was the creation of a network of community-based oral learning centers spread throughout the land. Each of the 12 tribes of Israel received an allotment of land as an inheritance, except one. The tribe of Levi received no lands but rather was granted cities spread throughout the rest of the tribes. This created a levitical priesthood that was essentially a national oral training system strategically distributed throughout the tribal lands. The nodes of the network totaled 48 Levitical cities established within the 12 tribes of Israel.[17] Its hub was first the Tabernacle in Shiloh and later the Temple in Jerusalem.

---

16 Dt 12:11
17 Nm 35

The levitical cities were positioned across the land in such a way that most Israelites were within half a day's walk from one of the cities, and no one was more than a day's journey away. It could be argued that it would have been more economical to have all the Levites resident around the Temple—it would certainly have saved in travel time and expense—but having them dispersed throughout the land was a very intentional part of God's training plan.

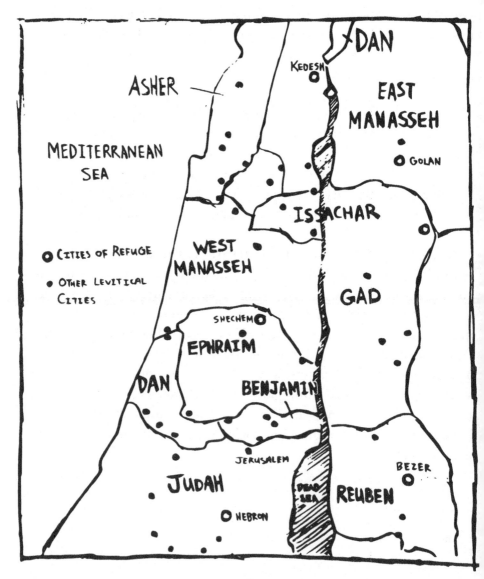

The Levites, who were responsible for the service of the Temple, were on a rotating schedule that took them regularly to Jerusalem for a given period of time before returning to their village until their next shift. While in Jerusalem, in addition to their work assignments they also benefitted from in-service training. The Levites studied the Word of God together in the Temple, and after learning in Jerusalem they returned to their cities where they passed on what they had learned to the tribal elders, who in turn passed it on to their communities.

One function of the levitical cities was to facilitate application of God's Word in everyday life; they were in many ways the equivalent of today's school system or radio and TV stations. The people would come to these urban centers for information, instruction and counsel on matters pertaining to practically every area of life: religious, medical, educational, legal and judicial, the settling of disputes and so forth. They would then go back home with the necessary information to share with their communities. It was a learn and share approach—their own adult education program.

Each of these three components—individual and family based engagement with God's Word, corporate learning events and community learning centers—was an essential part of God's oral educational methodology for the nation. It was systematic, comprehensive and inclusive, replicable and self-perpetuating.

God's strategy for his oral nation came with the promise that as he has given freedom from slavery in the past, we are continually given freedom from every kind of bondage. The verses that follow after the Sh'ma in Deuteronomy 6 are a straightforward explanation of God's intentions behind the specific laws he gave to his people, and the promise that comes with them:

In the future, when your son asks you, "What is the meaning of the stipulations, decrees and laws the Lord our God has commanded you?" tell him:

"We were slaves of Pharaoh in Egypt, but the Lord brought us out of Egypt with a mighty hand. Before our eyes the Lord sent signs and wonders—great and terrible—on Egypt and Pharaoh and his whole household. But he brought us out from there to bring us in and give us the land he promised on oath to our ancestors. The Lord commanded us to obey all these decrees and to fear the Lord our God, so that we might always prosper and be kept alive, as is the case today. And if we are careful to obey all this law before the Lord our God, as he has commanded us, that will be our righteousness."[18]

18 Dt 6: 20-25 NIV

Reflection Questions

1) Imagine a world without text; how would we learn and remember? How would we teach others?

2) When God chose the place for his dwelling to which Israel was to gather, the message was, "I am, and my word is, the final authority for life and practice." Where do we look to find the final authority today?

3) How does God's strategy with Israel inform our strategies among oral learners?

Chapter 4

Remember and Celebrate!

The Lord said to Moses, "Speak to the Israelites and say to them: 'These are my appointed festivals, the appointed festivals of the Lord, which you are to proclaim as sacred assemblies. There are six days when you may work, but the seventh day is a day of sabbath rest, a day of sacred assembly. You are not to do any work; wherever you live, it is a sabbath to the Lord. These are the Lord's appointed festivals, the sacred assemblies you are to proclaim at their appointed times.'"

– Leviticus 23: 1-4 NIV

Appointed festivals

The Lord is the inventor of great parties. God's oral strategy was to teach his people through celebration—events of joy for the whole community to actively participate in. Written into the very fabric of the Hebrew community was God's command to celebrate and remember. In this chapter, we will look specifically at how God gave the Hebrew people festivals of celebration to commemorate stories of what God had done in their history.

The festival calendar which God used with Israel was not only for them but is instructive for us today. God wants us to embody his joy in our daily lives. Daily, weekly and annual rhythms can help communities keep God's purposes and values before our hearts and minds. This is particularly true if the rhythms are enacted in ways that incorporate all our senses. If we understand the principles modeled in the festivals, we can apply their significance in creative and culturally appropriate ways in any context.

The Lord instructed the Israelites to gather in Jerusalem for three of these primary festivals during the course of the year: Pesach (Passover), Shavuot (Pentecost) and Sukkot (Feast of Tabernacles). Each festival had a story and ritual that gave the opportunity for learning and instilling God's character and values within each sector of society. Indeed, the Lord ordained celebration.

"Remembering" is a short film that considers how God reveals himself through biblical history and symbolism, depicting both ancient and modern rituals of celebration. Watch here:

https://master-storyteller.net/films/remembering

Pesach—celebrating freedom

There may be no other festival so rich in symbolism as the Passover (Pesach) in Hebrew tradition. The Pesach Seder, the meal and celebration that marks the start of the Passover, is a community event, in which whole families are transported back in time to reenact the experience of the story of Exodus—from slavery into freedom.

The name of the Passover meal is called *seder*, which means "order." The meal is a celebratory ritual that retells, through food and song, the story of Exodus in the proper "order"—a story that also reminds of the proper restoration of "order" to life. The table is set with elements that mark key points to remember in a particular order: bitter herbs that signify the bitterness of slavery, parsley dipped in salt water to remind participants of the tears shed, a shank bone to symbolize the lamb sacrificed the night the Hebrews fled, *charoset* (a mixture of nuts and apples made into a paste), and unleavened bread to symbolize how the Hebrews had to flee Egypt before they had time to let their bread rise. The last two elements are combined to make "sandwiches" that resemble the bricks and mortar that Hebrew slaves would make.

Following this feast of remembrance, for seven days the Israelites were to eat unleavened bread in a practice that still dominates the culture of today's global Jewish communities. For example, restaurants today switch to their "Passover" menu, while shops close down and shut off whole sections of leavened products. For seven days, a whole people group takes part in an observance that helps every person remember the story.

As Christians today, we are taught about the Lord's Supper and its significance for believers. We learn about how Jesus commanded this practice at his last meal with his disciples, which took place at Passover. But we rarely if ever learn or experience what a Passover celebration was actually like in Scripture. The beauty of the Passover celebration and its rich symbolism in every part of the food, song and "order" is a wonderful example of how richly integral the stories of Scripture can be to our lives if we enact them as a part of our communal practice.

Indeed, this Hebrew tradition can deepen our appreciation and understanding of Communion. Many of us don't realize that when we break the bread or sip the wine, that tradition is connected all the way back to the Old Testament, the time of Moses, and the salvation of the Israelites from slavery. So rich is the significance of the Passover that it was God's choice of symbol for His son's redemptive sacrifice, Jesus the "Passover Lamb." Jesus himself took the Pesach seder and instituted his own symbols in the practice that is called The Lord's Supper. Jesus' disciples understood the traditional symbolic significance of his instructions and actions during the Passover feast, Jesus' last meal. Then, after his death and resurrection, they understood that he himself was the sacrificial lamb who had been given as the sacrifice for the freedom of all. They understood that the blood of Jesus is like the blood of the Passover lamb, and that when the Almighty God sees the mark of blood on us, just like the doorposts in Egypt, he will pass over us, saving us from death.

God used the Passover festival and rituals to unify a nation, creating in them a corporate memory that was to be passed on to every addition to the community, whether the alien or the next generation. Beyond that, God used the Passover festival to create a collective consciousness that would prepare his people to understand the meaning of God's ultimate sacrifice. Jesus was sent *"first to the Jew"*[19] because these were the people whom God had prepared to understand the revelation of Messiah. He chose 12 Jewish disciples and later Saul of Tarsus around whom to build the Church because they had been given the foundation necessary to understand all that had been said about him in the Old Testament. They understood that Jesus was the fulfillment of the Scriptures, who came to give freedom to all people.

Shavuot—celebrating abundance

The feast of Shavuot (weeks) comes directly after the Passover celebration. After the Exodus from Egypt, God said:

---

19 Rom 1:16 NIV

...celebrate the Feast of Weeks to the Lord your God by giving a freewill offering in proportion to the blessings the Lord your God has given you. And rejoice before the Lord your God at the place he will choose as a dwelling for his Name—you, your sons and daughters, your male and female servants, the Levites in your towns, and the foreigners, the fatherless and the widows living among you. Remember that you were slaves in Egypt, and follow carefully these decrees. [20]

Shavuot is a harvest festival, a celebration of God's dwelling amongst his people, and his abundance and provision in community. In Scripture, the Israelites would bring the best of what they had from all over the nation—"first fruits" offerings—to the Temple, in a parade of song and joy.

Shavuot is also associated with the first giving of the law, and through the law God was highlighting relationship with himself and others. Although the Ten Commandments are commonly associated with do-nots, God used these and the rest of the detailed commands to show his people active ways of building a fruitful community; commands that said, "This is how you live together." This festival emphasizes an important precept of how God wanted his people to build community. The place where God would choose to associate his name would be a place where the rich and poor, relatives and servants, and even the foreigners and those generally marginalized in other societies joined together in unity. Everyone was to be welcomed into his place of dwelling. It was therefore important for all Israel to remember that they were slaves in Egypt and to not go back to the mentality of slavery, excluding others or treating them as unequal.

Further, in the New Testament, it was during the festival of Shavuot that God demonstrated the meaning of his place of dwelling. God used this feast with all the meaning it carried (his dwelling among us, first fruits and the receiving of the Law) and chose this to be the time when he would *"write the law on their hearts"* through the giving of the Holy Spirit,

---

20 Dt 16:10-12 NIV

as prophesied in Jeremiah 31.[21] Since this was a pilgrimage feast, everyone was to be there. As the Scripture says in Acts 2:1-11:

> *When the day of Pentecost came, they were all together in one place. Suddenly a sound like the blowing of a violent wind came from heaven and filled the whole house where they were sitting. They saw what seemed to be tongues of fire that separated and came to rest on each of them. All of them were filled with the Holy Spirit and began to speak in other tongues as the Spirit enabled them.*

> *Now there were staying in Jerusalem God-fearing Jews from every nation under heaven. When they heard this sound, a crowd came together in bewilderment, because each one heard their own language being spoken. Utterly amazed, they asked: "Aren't all these who are speaking Galileans? Then how is it that each of us hears them in our native language? Parthians, Medes and Elamites; residents of Mesopotamia, Judea and Cappadocia, Pontus and Asia, Phrygia and Pamphylia, Egypt and the parts of Libya near Cyrene; visitors from Rome (both Jews and converts to Judaism); Cretans and Arabs—we hear them declaring the wonders of God in our own tongues!*[22]

Not only did he make his dwelling among his disciples at this time, but he extended the invitation of himself to foreigners and spoke to them in their own languages. By understanding the feast of Shavuot, we can more fully grasp the power of the timing of the dispensation of the Holy Spirit. The Holy Spirit is a gift of the abundance of the Lord's presence, dwelling in and amongst us for every nation, tongue and tribe—excluding no one.

Sukkot—celebrating belonging

If you were told as a theology student today that God instituted camping as a way to teach His people dependence on Him, you might laugh at

---

21 Jer 31:33
22 Acts 2:1-11 NIV

the suggestion. But in Leviticus it is written plainly: *"You shall dwell in booths for seven days. All native Israelites shall dwell in booths, that your generations may know that I made the people of Israel dwell in booths when I brought them out of the land of Egypt: I am the Lord your God."*[23]

The people of Israel were nomads in the wilderness for forty years. During this time God sustained them and provided for them with food and shelter. He guided them with visible signs, and after forty years, they were finally brought to a permanent home. The feast of Sukkot (meaning tabernacles, tents, or booths) is a celebration of the provision and promise of the Lord, in providing the Israelites a continual home, even in the midst of a desert. In remembrance of their time in the wilderness, families were instructed to build their "booths" in a particular way using materials that also signify greater meaning.

The feast of Sukkot is still celebrated by the Jewish people today. If you were to walk around neighborhoods in Israel during the first evening of the feast, you might hear laughter and the smell of food. Families gather in temporary shelters, or "booths", put up next to homes and in gardens. The booths are decorated richly with colorful paper chains and ornaments. A table is put inside for the feast and mattresses lain on the floor for sleeping under the night sky. Every booth must have a portion that is open to the stars and a portion open to others or strangers. According to tradition, gazing at the heavens and seeing the stars should remind us of the majesty and awesomeness of our Creator. For seven days practicing families move outdoors for their meals, games and even sleeping. It is a joyous time of celebration and rest.

We can learn from the festival of Sukkot about the rituals God gave in Scripture to celebrate the sense of belonging he provides us, even as nomads in this world—a home amidst the desert. The entire story, and all the elements used, teach the lesson that God has gone before us to prepare a permanent dwelling—a land of promise. As with each festival, activities were both demonstrative and participatory in nature. They

---

23 Lv 23:42-43 ESV

engaged the entire community and all the senses through songs, food, objects, art and drama.

Sabbath—celebrating peace

In Jewish tradition, the Sabbath, or day of observance, begins as the sun sets on the Friday evening of every week. On the evening of the Sabbath, families gather together to share a meal, light candles and sing songs and prayers. This is the way that practicing Jewish people "welcome" the Sabbath. The purpose is to set aside a time to focus on relationship with God, family and community. Many families also disconnect from technology and work, instead fellowshipping with others and enjoying one another's company.

Shabbat Shalom is the phrase used to greet each other during the Sabbath. The translation is "Sabbath Peace." However this phrase encapsulates an even deeper meaning with the word shalom at its center—a joining together, wholeness, everything in right order. By wishing someone Shabbat Shalom the Sabbath's meaning of peace and righteousness is reinforced.

Through Shabbat, God draws us into his rest and his *shalom*, in relationship with himself and with one another. First, through right relationship and love with him, and then in extending ourselves in love to others, we bring about the celebration of shalom. In this way, the law of the Sabbath is not a "do-not-do" but a command "to do," a reminder to be fully present in relationship and also to reconcile and extend forgiveness, putting all into right order. The message of the Sabbath was not only communicated in the law, it was exemplified in nature. Leviticus 25 required the Israelites to have a "Sabbath Year" every seven years, which was a time for reconciling all areas of life: agriculture, finances and debt, employees and servants; in fact, all relationships. In the Sabbath year all debts were to be forgiven. This signifies release from striving and indebtedness to one another, a foreshadowing of an eternal shalom when all things will be completely made right with the Creator.

God instituted a system of festivals and rituals as part of his oral strategy to unify and give order to a nation. These rituals taught them about their relationship with the Lord and helped them to remember and recount his faithfulness. As they continued to experience God's miraculous interventions in their own times, the community created additional festivals and rituals. Dramas, games, songs and food were incorporated as means of conveying the story from one generation to another.

We can celebrate and worship God for what he has done for us not only in biblical times but in our own histories. Personal, family and community rituals, feasts and festivals can be created and practiced to instill into every generation the knowledge of God's faithfulness, and of his ways that bring freedom and abundant life. Will we take up the example and challenge of Scripture to practice God's Word orally, with our whole beings, in celebration and relationship with our communities?

Reflection Questions

1) How does the story of *Pesach* (Passover) deepen our understanding of Communion and why was a corporate memory important for Jesus to fulfill his purpose?

2) How does *Shavuot* (Weeks) enrich our understanding of Pentecost?

3) How has God used the festivals to build a common memory among his people? How might we celebrate this memory in active ways?

Chapter 5

Teaching without Words

And the LORD said to Moses, "Make a fiery serpent and set it on a pole, and everyone who is bitten, when he sees it, shall live." So Moses made a bronze serpent and set it on a pole. And if a serpent bit anyone, he would look at the bronze serpent and live.

– Numbers 21:8-9 ESV

guage of symbols

isually driven culture today, so much of our communication
igh symbols. We are accustomed to the meanings of a plethora
of logos and icons all around us. We have learned how effective these
symbols are in communicating quickly and powerfully. But in fact, many
of the symbols we use today have their roots in the Old Testament.

For example, one we might see everyday is the symbol of a snake on
a pole, known today as "The Rod of Asclepius." This symbol is most
commonly associated with the Greek Hippocrates, who was called the
"father of medicine," and is the most universal symbol of medicine
today. However, this same symbol traces back to a millennium earlier
than the ancient Greeks, when the Israelites were fleeing Egypt. As a
symbol of healing, created by God and used as a protection against
death, it was also well known at the time of Jesus, evident from when
he spoke in one of the greatest known verses in the New Testament:
*"As Moses lifted up the serpent in the wilderness, so must the Son of Man be
lifted up, that whoever believes in him may have eternal life. For God so loved
the world, that he gave his only Son, that whoever believes in him should not
perish but have eternal life."*[24]

God uses the language of symbols and symbolic acts as another method of
oral communication. From the rainbow to the cross—the Bible is saturated
with symbols. Studies in cultural memory show us that symbols have
the power to transcend national, linguistic and even cultural barriers.
Symbols have a language of their own. They have the power to speak
louder and say much more than many words could describe. Flags, for
instance, have the power to motivate, rally and inspire. Symbols make
us feel that we belong to something greater than ourselves, creating a
sense of identity, purpose and even destiny. In this chapter, we will look
at just a few of the significant symbols and symbolic acts God used in
the Old Testament. As we learn about these symbols, let's also consider

---

24 Jn 3:15-16 NIV

the ways in which we can symbolize the truth of God's Word in our oral cultures and communities today.

Symbols of the Tabernacle

Perhaps the most significant symbol to the Hebrew people was given to them in the wilderness. As the Hebrews left Egypt, they were destitute and terrified. They had left everything they owned and fled in the middle of the night. For over four hundred years they had been subject to slavery and brutal treatment. Suddenly they were on their own in the middle of a vast desert. They needed a sign that could be placed in the very heart of their community—a symbol which said to them: "I am with you."

The way God provided this was to invite them to build a dwelling for his presence. In Exodus 25, God gave Moses detailed instructions for the building of the Tabernacle, a symbol of the value of the Israelites' connection to their God. Every aspect and symbol of the Tabernacle was created according to the clear instruction from the Lord: *"And see that you make them after the pattern for them, which is being shown you on the mountain."*[25] The structure of the building itself was a visual message, and each object was a specific symbol with meaning.

---

25 Ex 25:40 ESV

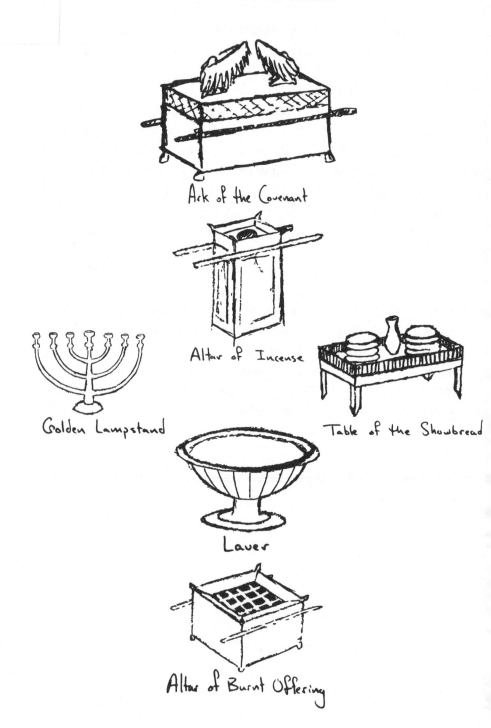

Ark of the Covenant

Altar of Incense

Golden Lampstand

Table of the Showbread

Laver

Altar of Burnt Offering

For instance, there was only one entrance into the outer courtyard surrounding the Tabernacle. In this outer courtyard was placed an "Altar of Burnt Offering." Without repentance and the appropriation of forgiveness through the the sacrifice of life it was not possible to enter further to worship. Next in the courtyard was the *Laver*, or basin, where the priests would wash with water before entering the Holy Place. This symbolized that after the justification that comes with the blood of the sacrificial lamb comes the washing with water (the root of the symbolic act of baptism). The Laver reminded the people that it is not enough to accept the atonement of the sacrifice, they also need to be sanctified and walk in purity to be in the presence of God.

Only after sacrifice and washing could they enter the interior. The interior was divided by a curtain separating the Holy Place and the Most Holy Place. Inside the Holy Place were the Golden Lampstand, the Table of the Showbread and the Altar of Incense.

"The Showbread" represented the Word of God. The meaning of the Hebrew words means the "bread of the face" or the "bread of the presence" and symbolized the presence of the Living Word. There were twelve loaves representing the twelve tribes of Israel, a reminder that not only the priests but all the people needed to embed God's words in their hearts and minds.

"The Golden Lampstand" was hammered out of one piece of pure gold. It consisted of a central shaft with six branches that extended from the trunk, three on each side. Each of the branches looked like those of an almond tree with buds, blossoms and flowers. The top of each flower was shaped into cups and filled with pure olive oil supplied by the priests who were commanded to keep the light burning continually. Olive oil was a symbol of the Holy Spirit and this oil was used to anoint kings at their commissioning.

The Lampstand also was used with the festival of Shavuot (Pentecost). In the second chapter of Acts, when the Holy Spirit was poured out at Pentecost, the disciples saw tongues of flame that came to rest upon each one of them. The symbolism would not have been lost upon the disciples. Just like the oil and the lamp stand, the New Testament teaches that it is the Holy Spirit who illuminates minds to see and understand God's word and ways. His light uncovers the secret places of the heart and convicts us of sin. His presence empowers his followers to *"walk in the light as he is in the light"*[26] and to live life more abundantly. Further, the six branches that held the oil correspond to the six fruits of the Spirit.

"The Altar of Incense" was the last of the articles in the Holy Place. The incense rose as a sweet fragrance before the presence of the Lord. On the Altar, incense was burnt twice a day: first, in the evening and then the morning. The New Testament refers to the prayers of the saints rising as incense before the Lord in four categories: petitions, prayers, intercessions and thanksgiving.[27]

Even the robe of the high priest was a symbol. The high priest's primary role was intercession—a constant prayer on behalf of the people. Every piece of the high priest's garment was pointing toward his intermediary role. The full garment consisted of a breastplate, robe and a "diadem," upon which was inscribed "Holy to God," so that God would graciously accept the people's sacrifices. On the ephod was embroidered twelve precious stones, inscribed with the names of the twelves tribes and which were called the "stones of reminder," believed to remind God of Israel. The high priest wore these garments on behalf of the Hebrew people and before God, turning him into a walking embodiment of the whole nation of Israel, each symbol carrying its own meaning.

Only the high priest could enter into the Most Holy Place, and only once a year on the Day of Atonement. Behind the veil, inside the Most Holy Place, was "the Ark of the Covenant" and the "Mercy Seat." The Ark of the Covenant contained the tablets of the Ten Commandments. The Mercy Seat was where the Glory of the Lord resided, and was on top of

---

26 I Jn 1:7 ESV

27 Rv 8:3-4

The Ark. The message of these two symbols is profound, communicating that God is a god whose character is fully both truth and grace, both justice and mercy. Yet, the Mercy Seat was above the tablets of the law. Indeed, as the disciple James communicated at a much later date, *"mercy triumphs over judgement."*[28] But this is only possible through the blood of the sacrifice.

There was much more symbolism that imbued every aspect of Tabernacle worship experience. But one of the most powerful symbols, hidden in the placement of the Tabernacle elements, could only be understood in hindsight—the positioning of the articles is in the shape of a cross. The master artist and designer carefully foreshadowed the death of the Messiah and underscored to his people that his dwelling place with man is laid upon the foundation of the cross.

28 Jas 2:13 ESV

The symbols of the Tabernacle and the robes of the high priest tell a complete story of sacrifice and redemption. Using this rich pictorial understanding, the prophets could explain the complex principles of salvation and forgiveness. The following words used by the prophet Isaiah all symbolically point to articles from the Tabernacle:

> *The Spirit of the Lord God is upon me,*
> *because the Lord has anointed me...*
> *... to grant to those who mourn in Zion—*
> *to give them a beautiful headdress instead of ashes,*
> *the oil of gladness instead of mourning,*
> *the garment of praise instead of a faint spirit...*[29]

Jesus chose to read this passage in the synagogue when he visited his hometown in Nazareth saying, *"Today this scripture is fulfilled in your hearing,"* proclaiming himself as the great high priest.[30] Later he also referred to the bread in the Tabernacle when he said, *"man shall not live by bread alone but by every word that proceeds from the mouth of God."*[31] The Hebrew people understood from the Tabernacle that God's Word was the bread of life. Jesus was saying that the showbread represents his person, presence and body and that he and his Word are life and sustenance. The Book of Romans also tells us that Jesus is the great high priest, interceding on our behalf before the Father.[32]

Rituals as symbolic acts

Just as God reveals himself through the depth of meaning in symbols, he initiated active ways of coming into his presence—rituals that underscore the establishment of his relationship and promises with his people. Entering the presence of God required repentance and sacrifice, tangible covenants, and rites of passage.

---

29 Is 61:1-3 ESV
30 Lk 4:21 NIV
31 Mt 4:4 NKJV
32 Rom 8:34

Sacrifice: the symbolic act of repentance

In Hebrew, *korban* refers to the object of the sacrifice: the animal or other item to be sacrificed. The root word for korban is *karev*, meaning "bring near." There are a number of Hebrew words that derive from this root, including words that mean bringing a sacrifice, to come near, a close relative and even a telescope.

The sacrifice ritual conveyed relationship with God at each point in its process and through every element. The act of taking a perfect and valuable lamb from the flock, laying hands on it, slaughtering it and then burning portions on the altar involved the senses of sight, sound, smell and touch. The sense of taste was involved as the participants ate the meat of the sacrifice. The process could not help but evoke an emotional response. Family and community participation had seared onto their minds and souls the fact that sin is costly—that life and relationship come with a price. Yet, as they ate the meat of the sacrifice they realized that the ultimate goal was the restoration of right relationship with God, and that with that restoration came the joy of communion over a meal. At the heart of the ritual of sacrifice is the promise of drawing near to God.

Covenants: to cut a contract

Whether it was with God or with other people, entering into a covenant was an extensive ritual often involving sacrifice, and included a visual or tangible representation. We see this in the story of Jacob, when after leaving home to seek a wife, he had a vision of a ladder to heaven. There he entered into a covenant with God and set up a pillar as a sign of the covenant. Upon his return 20 years later, when Jacob and Laban joined in a covenant of peace, they sealed their promise with sacrifices. Once again a pillar of stones was used as a visual representation of their covenant to all who saw it.

The Hebrew wording for "making covenant" is much stronger and more graphic than the English suggests. These words, *karat berit*, literally mean "to cut a covenant." While other words are sometimes used in

Scripture, *karat* occurs 90 times. The Jewish people were required to make a physical "cut" on the males as a physical sign, symbolizing their covenant faithfulness to God.

At Mount Sinai before the building of the Tabernacle, Israel "cut a covenant" as a confirmation of the laws given by God, and as a promise to be a kingdom of priests and a holy nation. They did so with an intense ceremony involving water purification and blood sacrifice, and when the elders were invited to draw near to God, they entered into fellowship and communion with him. Moses then took the blood, sprinkled it on the people and said, *"This is the blood of the covenant that the Lord has made with you in accordance with all these words."*[33]

Baptism: a rite of passage

The ritual of water purification that was carried into generations of Hebrew tradition is called *mikveh*. Pilgrims were required to wash in baptismal pools before they could enter the courts of the Temple or the presence of God. They could only wash in "living" or running water, usually from a stream or spring, to provide purification and healing. Every part of the pilgrim's body had to be fully submerged in this water.

John the Baptist utilized this practice, baptizing those who responded to his message of repentance and came to be washed clean of their sins in the River Jordan. When the apostles were sent out they continued this tradition. After Jesus' resurrection, baptism came to be understood as a symbol of identifying with the death and resurrection of Christ, the "living water" who brings purification before God. This was a symbolic rite of passage from a kingdom of darkness to a kingdom of light. John records Jesus saying, *"...unless one is born of water and the Spirit, he cannot enter the kingdom of God."*[34]

---

33 Ex 24:8 NIV
34 Jn 3:5 ESV

As Paul writes in Colossians,

> *In him also you were circumcised with a circumcision made without hands, by putting off the body of the flesh, by the circumcision of Christ, having been buried with him in baptism, in which you were also raised with him through faith in the powerful working of God, who raised him from the dead.*[35]

Names as symbols of promise
"As his name is, so is he."[36]

A name signifies identity and was used in the Bible as a continual marker over an individual's life. In a powerful address to foreigners and eunuchs who hold fast to his covenants, God says in Isaiah 56:5, *"To them I will give in my house and within my walls a memorial, and a name better than that of sons and daughters; I will give them an everlasting name which will not be cut off."*[37]

Naming in Hebrew tradition is a hugely symbolic action, and often the experience of the name-giver creates the name. Abraham, for example, named his son Isaac, meaning "laughter," because when Sarah found out that God had promised her a son when old and barren, she laughed. The act of renaming is similar, occurring in significant places throughout Scripture. Each time someone is renamed by God in the Bible, they have had an encounter with him, and from that moment forward, their life is new. The ritual of renaming symbolizes leaving the old, cutting off the things that are apart from God, and coming into a newness of purpose and calling.

In Hebrew, Abram means high or exalted father. When God made a covenant with Abram he said, *"No longer will you be called Abram; your name will be Abraham, for I have made you a father of many nations."*[38] The

---

35 Col 2:11-12 ESV
36 1 Sm 25:25 ESV
37 Is 56:5 NASB
38 Gn 17:5 NIV

new promise came with a new identification. Abraham's wife Sarai, meaning "my sorrow," was renamed Sarah as a symbol of hope, denoting her as a "princess," the mother of nations, when she received the promise of Isaac's birth.

Abraham's grandson, Jacob, was named a word meaning "one who follows" or "supplanter." He was born grabbing at his brother Esau's heel, and although he was weaker, he used his cunning to "supplant" Esau twice, once for his birthright and once for his blessing. Then, after he wrestled with the angel, he was told, *"Your name will no longer be Jacob, but Israel, because you have struggled with God and with humans, and have overcome."*[39] That encounter transformed him from "supplanter" to "prevails with God," or in some translations, "overcomes with God." He may have been left with a limp for the rest of his life, but he had also earned a new name and inheritance. Jacob realized that he had encountered God, so he also named the place of occurrence as significant: *"Then Jacob asked him and said, 'Please tell me your name.' But he said, 'Why is it that you ask my name?' And he blessed him there. So Jacob named the place Peniel [the face of God], for he said, 'I have seen God face to face, yet my life has been preserved.'"*[40]

In the New Testament, Simon Peter was renamed when he acknowledged Jesus as God. He stood face to face with him and Jesus said, *"Blessed are you, Simon Bar-Jonah! For flesh and blood has not revealed this to you, but my Father who is in heaven. And I tell you, you are Peter [Rock], and on this rock I will build my church, and the gates of hell shall not prevail against it."*[41] This name came with a new calling and destiny. Despite his recognition of Jesus as Messiah, Peter still walked through some days of wavering and doubt, but then stepped into his calling with boldness and declared the new kingdom to thousands in Jerusalem on the day of Pentecost.

---

39 Gn 32:28 NIV
40 Gn 29-30 NASB
41 Mt 16:17-18 ESV

Jerusalem: city of shalom
As people of God in the world, we are called to live by otherworldly standards. We believe this choice will ultimately transform the current realities around us. Jerusalem symbolizes this in its name. The Hebrew *Yeru-shalem* is a play on words. *Yeru* means "they will see," and *Ir* means "city." The Hebrew word shalom, meaning "peace" comes from the root *shalem*, which means "whole" or "complete." In this play on words Jerusalem can mean "city of shalom" or "they will see shalom." The biblical concept of wholeness is when everything is in right order. And when all is in right order the result is peace. Jesus, called the Prince of Peace, shed his blood so that everything in heaven and on earth may be reconciled and put in right order under God.

The Bible refers to Jerusalem as the "city of the great king," the Messiah. The New Jerusalem foretold in the Revelation is the city where God rules and is eternally present. There are no tears, no sorrow, and only peace, for there is no longer brokenness. And "those who overcome" will each be given a new name, written in stone.[42] God tells us to give him no rest until Jerusalem is established as a praise in the earth. Jerusalem is a call for God's people to live toward a vision, seeing that which is not yet, because they believe him who has promised to make all things new. *"He who overcomes, I will make him a pillar in the temple of My God, and he will not go out from it anymore; and I will write on him the name of My God, and the name of the city of My God, the new Jerusalem, which comes down out of heaven from My God, and My new name."*[43]

These are just a few of the symbols and symbolic acts the Lord gave us in Scripture to communicate more of his character and desire for relationship with us. God does not take any aspect of his communication lightly, as evidenced by the intricacy of his symbolic designs. The Creator

---

42 Rv 2:17
43 Rv 3:12 NASB

of the universe did not write words hidden in an obscure text. The Lord is the master communicator who gives meaning and speaks through every detail. We are the ones who limit him. How might we embrace the manifold symbolism of the Lord in how we communicate and listen every day? Do we expect the Lord to speak through symbols, signs and wonders? As Malcolm Muggeridge famously said, "Every happening, great and small, is a parable whereby God speaks to us, and the art of life is to get the message."[44]

Reflection Questions

1) How does God engage all the senses in the symbolism he uses in the Scriptures discussed? How can we likewise engage all the senses when communicating who God is with others?

2) How does Jesus fulfill the symbolic role of the high priest?

3) How can we follow the example of the Lord by using symbols, rituals and names to communicate truth in our contexts?

---

44 Malcolm Muggeridge, *Christ and the Media* (Vancouver: Regent College Publishing 2003) 25

Chapter 6

God Speaks to the Heart

The voice of the Lord is over the waters;
the God of glory thunders,
the Lord thunders over the mighty waters.
The voice of the Lord is powerful;
the voice of the Lord is majestic.

— Psalm 29:3-4 NIV

God is a singer

All of us have likely had an experience in which a song or melody has impacted us beyond words. Songs speak to the heart and to the spirit, passing through our barriers, reaching our core. Music and poetry have been used from the beginning of time in powerful ways, whether as an expression of love, lament, worship, celebration, or even leading warriors into battle with songs of declaration. Music is one of the languages of God, and God is a singer, speaking and calling to us in song—"*deep calls to deep*"[45]—connecting to the parts of us that sometimes lay beneath our everyday lives.

God sings his promises over his people. In the same way that he gave symbols of redemption for them to remember, he uses song to emphasize his faithfulness and gift of hope. God is an oral communicator, filling his Word with poetry and song.[46] He sings, and through poetry and allegory gives his people revelation of himself. In oral tradition, these poems were usually set to music, and the Hebrew oral tradition of singing the words of the prophets and psalms continues today. In this chapter, we will explore how God calls us into worship through music and poetry, and how he uses this communal oral practice to help us remember who he is from generation to generation.

Calling us to worship

A harmonious symphony rings out in every aspect of creation, saying "yes" and "amen!" with praises to the Creator. The prophets and the psalmists were inspired by this beautiful noise rising up from the earth, a song that echoes the voice of the Lord Himself. The psalmist, King David, a musician himself, appointed Levites as worshippers to minister daily around the Ark of the Covenant. He told them how to worship, saying,

---

45 Ps 42:7 ESV

46 Mark E. Wenger, "Poetry and the Bible, an Introduction (Lecture notes)," *Columbia International University*, accessed August 15, 2017, http://www.academia.edu/7110653/ Poetry_and_the_Bible_-_An_Introduction_Lecture_Notes_).

"Sing to the Lord all the earth, proclaim his salvation day after day. Declare his glory among the nations, his marvelous deeds among all peoples."[47] He goes on to instruct a calling to creation, where all mankind and nature join together in song to their Creator: *"Let the heavens rejoice, let the earth be glad; let them say among the nations, 'The Lord reigns!' Let the sea resound, and all that is in it; let the fields be jubilant, and everything in them! Let the trees of the forest sing, let them sing for joy before the Lord."*[48]

The Psalms repeatedly exalt worship and meditation day and night. Meditation is dwelling in the truth and internalizing who God is. The center of every assembly event in Hebrew tradition is worship and meditation of Scripture through song. Further, God uses allegory and metaphor in poetry to describe himself. These descriptions move us beyond what we can experience in the natural, taking us into the realm of the imagination and inspiring worship.

Love, lament, war and celebration

God's voice not only inspires worship. His Word has many themes of love and lament that his people expressed through songs and poetry. Song of Songs is entirely composed of poetic expressions of love and intimacy in relationship. Nearly half of the Psalms (73 of 150) include the essential element for lament: the prayerful plea to God for help. Scripture also records many songs of victory, deliverance and celebration. Moses and the Israelites, after passing through the Red Sea, sang a song together, and Miriam gathered the Israelite women in songs and a dance of celebration: *"Sing to the LORD, for he is highly exalted. Both horse and driver he has hurled into the sea."*[49]

One of the most stirring stories of victory in the Old Testament takes place when Jehoshaphat was King of Judah and the Israelites were at war with their surrounding enemies. The King received a prophecy that

---

47 1 Ch 16:23-24 NIV
48 1 Ch 16:31-33 NIV
49 Ex 15:21 NIV

the Lord would fight the battle for them, and that they were to go as an army to "stand still and see" the Lord's hand at work. After consulting the people, Jehoshaphat appointed men to sing to the Lord and to praise him for the splendor of his holiness as they went out at the head of the army, saying: *"Give thanks to the Lord, for his love endures forever."*[50] As they began to sing and praise, the Lord set ambushes against the men of Ammon and Moab and Mount Seir who were invading Judah, and they were defeated.

The Israelites chose to have faith and believe God even before their victory was won. The songs of praise, declaring who God is, were the first and most important act in the battle. Not only does this story show the importance of worship and belief, it also shows the principle of winning the battle in our minds before winning the battle in reality. Singing and speaking out truth can quiet our fears and give courage to our hearts.

Jesus grew up in the Hebrew culture where songs were a collective tradition, and he himself sang songs of worship and deliverance. Hebrews 2:12 refers to Jesus saying, *"I will declare your name to my brothers and sisters; in the assembly I will sing your praises,"*[51] and at the end of his Last Supper, or Passover meal with his disciples, he sang a hymn of praise with them. Jesus was and is the chief musician.

Songs to remember

Take a moment and think about your favourite songs growing up—songs you might have even learned before you could read. How many lyrics can you remember? Did you ever see them *written down*? Yet our memories retain them far better than any long section of prose or writing. "Oral Literature," comprised of epics, ballads, prose tales, ritual and lyric songs have been passed down from generation to generation before writing was even invented. These forms that combine lyrics with rhythm, repetition and melody have aided communities to pass complex information without the need for written words.

---

50 2 Ch 20:21 NIV
51 Heb 2:12 NIV

All songs and poems in Scripture are used to communicate, teach and *remember*. Moses wrote a song he taught to all the people. He told them: *"Now therefore write this song and teach it to the people of Israel. Put it in their mouths, that this song may be a witness for me against the people of Israel...this song shall confront them as a witness (for it will live unforgotten in the mouths of their offspring)."*[52]

Moses was explicit that this song would live longer than the next generation, and he was right—it even makes an appearance in the Book of Revelation, where those who have overcome sing the same song: *"They held harps given them by God and sang the song of God's servant Moses and of the Lamb."*[53]

Another song refrain that was passed down from the time of Moses through generations are the words, *"The Lord is gracious and merciful, slow to anger and abounding in steadfast love."*[54] This refrain entered into the corporate identity of the Hebrew people as words they would have sung together—words that built their common knowledge of who God is. We see them as a thread through the Old Testament, and have likely ascribed them to King David, Asaph or the other great psalmists. However, in Exodus 34:6-7 we learn that they were spoken by God Himself. God revealed Himself to Moses, proclaiming, *"The Lord, the Lord, the compassionate and gracious God, slow to anger, abounding in love and faithfulness, maintaining love to thousands, and forgiving wickedness, rebellion and sin."*[55] What started off as God's words, revealing his character to Moses on Mount Sinai, soon began to inspire a community's learning through the Psalms, and even today form part of songs that are sung in worship to Him in many different languages across the globe.

---

52 Dt 31:19-21 ESV
53 Rv 15:2-4 NIV
54 Ps 145:8 ESV
55 Ex 34:6-7 NIV

Similarly, one of the most repeated refrains in the Bible is often translated *"his love (or mercy) endures forever."* This refrain appears at least 44 times across the Old Testament: it appears as a repeated line in Psalm 136 which tells the story of creation, the Passover and other key moments in Israel's history. David uses the oral cultural form of call and answer to repeat this refrain after each line, emphasizing how each part of the story teaches of God's unending mercies. This is a wonderful example of story, song and repetition working together to help an oral people learn truths about their Creator and Sustainer in a way they can remember.

Walter Ong, the author of *Orality and Literacy,* says that in a primary oral culture if knowledge is not repeated over and over again, then this knowledge will vanish quickly.[56] What we are discovering through science, oral communities have known and practiced for centuries: poetry and songs help us remember.

God is surrounded by a host of singing angels amidst a singing creation, and we are also called to sing so as to remember and rejoice in who God is with our whole beings. The Apostle Paul, though highly educated and textually literate, understood that through song a barely literate community could memorize and internalize the Word of God. His words instruct us: *"Let the word of Christ dwell in you richly, teaching and admonishing one another in all wisdom, singing psalms and hymns and spiritual songs, with thankfulness in your hearts to God."*[57]

---

56 Walter J. Ong, *Orality and Literacy*, (New York: Routledge, 2002), 40.
57 Col 3:16 ESV

Reflection Questions

1) What is a song you carry in your heart and how did you learn it?

2) What is the value of songs, music, and poetry as seen in Hebrew tradition?

3) How can we use music and poetry to instill the character of the Lord in our cultures?

Chapter 7

When God Shouts

Miracles are a retelling in small letters of the very same story which is written across the whole world in letters too large for some of us to see.

– C.S. Lewis, God in the Dock

To this point we have seen that God has communicated orally through the wonders of nature, through stories, symbols, artifacts and songs, as well as through community learning and cultural events. All of these can be put into the category of what we think of as normal and natural. God has used every "normal" means possible to communicate with humankind. But the normal has not always been enough. At times God has had to raise his voice and shout in order to get our attention.

Throughout human history God has used supernatural means, at times even contravening the laws of nature which he has established, in order to communicate with us. Countless books could be written about God's supernatural interventions in history. In this chapter, we will look at just a few examples of the supernatural methods God has used to communicate.

Dreams, visions, and interpretations

Dreams and visions are another of God's ways of getting through to us; they bypass normal thought patterns, providing a picture or a story that communicates beyond our rational processes. Throughout the Old Testament period the judges and prophets of Israel received divine instructions and revelations through God-given visions; this was accepted as a normal way of God's communication in Hebrew tradition.

This did not change in New Testament times: the shape of the early Church was largely directed by visions. The early Church fathers experienced one of the most dramatic shifts in understanding as a result of two visions. The first came to Cornelius, a God-fearing Roman centurion, and the second to the Apostle Peter. As each obeyed the direction which God gave him in his vision, the course of Church history was radically changed, so much so that today we still experience the ripple effect of that tidal wave.[58]

Further, much of the biblical account of the growth of the Church beyond Jerusalem is traced back to two other visions: the first revealed to

---

58 Acts 10

Saul of Tarsus, and the second to Ananias. The vision given to Ananias commanded a perilous task: lead Saul to faith. However, Ananias took this risk in obedience, and now nearly half of the books in the New Testament are attributed to this Jewish man Saul, whom we know as Paul. In his ministry, Paul speaks of visions and revelations received while he was transported to the third heaven.[59] These revelations became part of the foundation of his ministry and teaching.

Similarly, God communicated orally with John in a prophetic vision which we call the Revelation. That vision is foundational to our understanding of end times and to the hope we hold of the ultimate triumph of good over evil. That hope serves as a central motivation for discipleship and obedience to God's ways. Peter, Paul and John were perhaps the most influential leaders of the early Church movement, contributing approximately three quarters of the New Testament. And the messages that God communicated to these individuals orally through visions still prevails two thousand years into the present, where it stands as the foundation of present day Christianity.

Angels
Angels are God's envoys used when he wants to communicate something special—an angelic visitation is God's exclamation mark. Angels are mentioned 273 times in the Bible (108 in the Old Testament and 165 in the New Testament) and appear consistently throughout Scripture, from the Garden of Eden to the Revelation. The messenger Gabriel appeared to Daniel and spoke with him concerning current and future events. Gabriel later appeared to Mary to tell her the Holy Spirit would come upon her, and she would have a child, and he would be called the son of God. No one who has seen an angel could mistake their message as a mental illusion.

Audible voice
There is a long list of people who heard God speaking to them throughout Scripture. Whether this was a voice they heard with their ears or just in

---

59 2 Co 12

their minds is not always clear from the context, but we do know that God's voice was not just textual. God speaks audibly. His voice is not a passing whim or delusion. His voice is clear, consistent and true.

The account of God's redemptive strategy in human history begins in the Garden, but it takes on new dimensions when God speaks to a man telling him to leave his home and relatives and to embark upon a journey into the unknown. Abraham's journey and subsequent steps taken in obedience to the voice he heard have resulted in blessings to the entire human race. By way of them we have received both the Bible and the Messiah.

Samuel was a man who definitely heard God speak in an audible voice. As a child serving Eli the priest in the Tabernacle, when he *"did not yet know the Lord, neither was the word of the Lord yet revealed to him,"*[60] God called his name while he lay in bed. This happened three times and each time Samuel replied, *"here I am."* Finally, the Lord came and stood by him and called out, *"Samuel, Samuel."* This time Samuel answered, *"speak Lord for your servant hears."*

God also spoke with an audible voice at the Baptism of Jesus. A voice from heaven was heard saying *"This is my beloved Son, in whom I am well pleased."*[61]

Interventions in nature
God communicates by intervening in nature and doing what we think of as impossible.

In Exodus, when Moses was herding sheep in the desert he saw a bush burning, and yet the fire did not consume it. God caused Aaron's staff to turn into a snake before Pharaoh. He showed his authority clearly when he sent plagues that humbled the strongest nation on earth, and in bringing these plagues through Moses he authenticated Moses' position

---

60 1 Sam 3:7 KJV
61 Mt 3:17 ASV

as leader of the people of Israel. The parting of the Red Sea told Israel that God was their deliverer even in the face of the greatest odds, and the daily manna and water in the desert echoed his promise of provision. He caused Aaron's rod to bud as a sign that God had chosen him and the tribe of Levi to be priests before the Lord. The budding rod was then kept as a graphic memorial in the Tabernacle.[62]

Throughout Scripture, God continuously communicated through supernatural acts in the environment to show his provision and power. He caused the sun to stand still and even to move ten degrees backward in the sky.[63] Fire fell from heaven to consume not only the prophet's sacrifice but the stones of the altar and the water-filled trough surrounding it.[64] City walls fell down at the sound of trumpets and entire armies were blinded and caused to surrender to a defenseless people.[65] At the time of the crucifixion, when the veil to the Holy of Holies was torn in two, the earth shook and the sky turned dark through midday.[66] The examples of God's interventions in nature go on and on. The Lord expressed his power and sovereignty both through nature and by contravening the laws of nature.

Signs and wonders

Miracles are another way in which God raises his voice to gain our attention. Can a grown man or woman be created without a mother? Can an 80 year old woman who has never been able to conceive give birth? Can a virgin have a son? Can a man be thrown into a fiery furnace and survive unscathed? Can the blind be made to see, the deaf to hear and the lame to walk? Can the dead rise to life? The answer to every one one of these questions is a resounding yes! Each one stems from a biblical account, and each makes a strong statement about the nature, character and ways of God. When Jesus healed the shriveled arm of the

---

62 Ex 3-16
63 Is 38:8
64 1 Kgs 18:38
65 Jo 6:20; 2 Kgs 6:18
66 Mt 27:45-51

man in the synagogue, he did so in order that the people would know that he was Lord of the Sabbath.[67] The message of the Gospel and the ministries of Peter, John and Paul were frequently authenticated by miraculous healings. To the Corinthians Paul said, *"My message and my preaching were not with wise and persuasive words, but with a demonstration of the Spirit's power..."*[68] Miracles make the invisible God visible. What we observe with our senses and experience in our persons is hard to refute or to forget.

So many more stories of God's supernatural "show and tell" could be recounted. Time and space fail us, as it would take an entire Bible in order to tell the multiple ways in which God has communicated orally through supernatural acts of wonder. All that we consider normal is but a passing shadow of what is truly real, a finite reflection of the greatness and glory of God, the fullness of which is yet to be revealed to those who hear and believe. God intervenes in a way that inspires faith—an unmistakable expression of himself that lets his people know they have encountered God.

---

67 Mt 12:10-13
68 I Cor 2:4 NIV

Reflection Questions

1) Why does God use miracles as a key part of his strategy for revealing himself?

2) What are ways that God shouts in our lives today?

3) In what ways is it hard for our community to believe in and perceive the supernatural power of the Lord in our lives? How can we receive and perceive God's miracles more?

Chapter 8

Stories Beyond the Ordinary

*Tell me a fact and I will learn it. Tell me a truth and I will believe it.
Tell me a story and it will live in my heart forever.*

– Native American proverb

Storytelling is oral tradition

Story is central to all of us because it is a bridge to the heart. Stories have shaped us and given us the willingness to believe, to dare, to risk, to venture beyond our comfort zones. When they are based in the truth of human experience they are repeated, told and retold in new ways and in various mediums, shaping culture. And of course the greatest and longest lasting stories come from the greatest author.

Bible stories have captured our imaginations and helped us to understand that obedience to God's call is to be sought over comfort, and that service to the world is more important than riches. In fact, it is what makes us rich. Whether it is hearing about Daniel in the den of lions, Ruth and Naomi, or Jonah and the whale—stories fashion our understanding of God and his faithfulness. In this chapter we will explore the power of the biblical custom of storytelling.

From generation to generation

One of the most poignant and emotionally gripping stories of Scripture is that of Abraham and the sacrifice of Isaac. *"As the two of them went on together, Isaac spoke up and said to his father Abraham, 'Father?' 'Yes, my son?' Abraham replied. 'The fire and wood are here,' Isaac said, 'but where is the lamb for the burnt offering?'"*[69]

We can perhaps feel the bewilderment of the child Isaac and the pain of Abraham. We can begin to comprehend the agonizing choice of the heavenly Father. In the extension of the story, God sees Abraham's obedience, and gives him a lamb to sacrifice instead of Isaac. Abraham was told by God that as a result of his faith and obedience he would become the father of many nations; in fact that all nations would be blessed because he obeyed God's voice. This story displays many dimensions of the character of God. It also teaches us the meaning of obedience, its costs and rewards, and the implications not only to immediate family but to unborn generations.

---

69 Gn 22:6-7 NIV

The story told and retold has shaped a people and a religion. It has given them a sense of belonging, place and destiny, and it reaches far beyond even the original people through whom it was first recounted. Abraham's story foreshadowed another story of even greater sacrifice that took place on the very same mountain and through which people from nearly every nation have come to be spiritual descendants of Abraham. This story of the greatest sacrifice of the Father giving his Son is living, and is actively shaping and reshaping families, cultures and peoples around the globe at this very moment.

The storytelling king

The oral tradition throughout Scripture is primarily one of storytelling. King Solomon was an example of a prolific storyteller. He *"spoke three thousand proverbs and his songs numbered a thousand and five."*[70] His wisdom was conveyed through proverbs and songs. Leaders of the nations came to *listen* to Solomon's wisdom. The Queen of Sheba declared, *"How happy your officials, who continually stand before you and hear your wisdom!"*[71] The whole world sought audience with Solomon to *hear* the wisdom God had put in his heart. Solomon, a highly literate king, who was also a scientist, an architect, a composer and one of the wisest men of all time, chose to use story forms and songs as his preferred method of communication.

In telling stories, Jesus continued the oral customs of the prophets and Kings recorded in the Old Testament. Jesus was the master of story. He told parables using stories that were very familiar to the local people because they were taken from their everyday experience. He drew examples from their work tending vineyards, shepherding the flocks, fishing with nets, and even preparing bread. The allegories in his parables that seem so obscure to a modern western culture would have been completely relevant to the local people.

Matthew, one of Jesus' 12 closest followers, stated that Jesus spoke to the multitudes of people that came to hear him using parables, and without

70 1 Kgs 4:32 NIV
71 1 Kgs 10:8 NIV

65

a parable he did not speak to them.[72] The Gospels record 46 different parables told by Jesus but also state that he told many other stories.[73] Jesus often answered questions with a story so that people could go deeper and grapple with the application of the truth. If he had just answered out of his knowledge the people would not have had to "own" their own response or see their own lives in contrast. By speaking in parables, Jesus gives enough revelation for anyone to come to him, while allowing people to grapple with the story so as to apply the truth more deeply.

One of the most famous of Jesus' stories is that of The Good Samaritan in Luke 10. The account begins with a lawyer asking Jesus what he must do to inherit eternal life. Jesus responds by asking a question: *"What is written in the law? How do you understand it?"*[74]

The man replied by quoting what was perhaps the best known Scripture passage to the Jewish audience who was present: *"You shall love the Lord your God with all your heart and with all your soul and with all your strength and with all your mind, and your neighbor as yourself."*[75] The man proceeded to inquire, *"and who is my neighbor?"*[76]

It was then that Jesus told the story of a man who was robbed and beaten and left along the road to die. Religious people on their way to the Temple in Jerusalem who saw the man were afraid to get involved, as it would not only delay them but make them unclean before entering the Temple. Only the Samaritan (an outcast according to their tradition) tended to him and personally paid for his care until he recovered.

Jesus then asked the lawyer, and indirectly everyone listening, *"which of these three do you think was a neighbor to the man who fell into the hands of robbers?"*[77] In other words, who was the true inheritor of eternal life?

---

72 Mt 13:34
73 Mk 4:33-34
74 Lk 10:26 NET
75 Lk 10:27 ESV
76 Lk 10:29 ESV
77 Lk 10:36 NIV

Jesus was drawing his listeners into an understanding of the Kingdom by telling them about a situation that pitted religious tradition against compassion. The Pharisees during Jesus' time wanted actions to repeat, to follow and monitor, but Jesus told of a kingdom that was not static.

Why did Jesus rely on storytelling? In the fictional satire, *The Screwtape Letters*, C.S. Lewis writes from the voice of a senior demon to his nephew about the "strategies" of the Enemy (God):

> *But you now see that the Irresistible and the Indisputable are the two weapons which the very nature of His scheme forbids Him to use. Merely to override a human will (as His felt presence in any but the faintest and most mitigated degree would certainly do) would be for Him useless. He cannot ravish. He can only woo.*[78]

Jesus woos us, and through poetry and storytelling brings us into discovery. He gives us an invitation to participate, calling us to become part of the story and make it our own.

The theater of storytelling

We often think of storytelling in oral tradition as only speech or audio. But biblical storytelling was theatrical. In order to reach their audiences leaders and prophets were often sensational. As much as 70 percent of Scripture is narrative and poetry, which lends itself well to oral communication in theater. Paul's epistles fall within the remaining 30 percent. Yet what we often do not realize is that these too were conveyed in an oral manner to the original audience. The letters were not only shared and taught, but acted out and demonstrated.

Paul exhorts the leadership in Thessalonica to make sure that his letter is read in the hearing of the entire fellowship of believers. It was the usual practice in the early church that letters were read aloud to the whole assembly.[79] The receiving fellowship would gather and the content of

---

78 C.S. Lewis, *The Screwtape Letters* (New York: Harper Collins, 2001), 39
79 Col 4:16; Rev 1:3

the letter was then shared verbally and theatrically with the listeners. The listeners were themselves active participants interacting with the content, its meaning and application.[80]

The dramatic delivery of storytelling began early in the Old Testament through the prophets. Scholars studying the culture of the ancient Middle East believe that the prophets performed their stories with great drama to command their audiences. Even before the prophets, we see indications of this with Moses and Aaron asking God for signs so that the people would listen. Elijah and Elisha displayed spectacular miracles and saw prayers answered before crowds of people. The prophets used the wind and sky or rivers and fire as props in their delivery.

In *Prophets as Performers*, Terry Giles writes,

> *The prophetic performer asks the audience to imagine reality differently—to see through the prophet's eyes. With practiced skill, the prophet draws his audience into the alternate world of his drama by weaving together the familiar and the unexpected, creating a series of reversals that open the audience to alternative social possibilities... Through his oration, the prophetic performer moves his audience past appearances, behind the everyday and familiar... Rather, the prophet leads his audience to imagine a world that could be...*[81]

Similarly, Jesus plays the role of the ultimate prophetic performer. Not only did he use the everyday understanding of his audience as he told his story, he performed miracles before the people, while using as his theater set the "props" around him—the vineyard, the olive press and other objects from life and nature. He opened our imaginations to a whole new world.

---

80 P.H. Davids, (presentation, Houston, 2015).

81 Terry Giles, "Prophets as Performers," *Bibleodyssey.org*, accessed August 28, 2017, https://www.bibleodyssey.org/en/passages/related-articles/prophets-as-performers

The basis of oral tradition, and indeed of Scripture, is storytelling. Facts and figures can be distorted, taken out of context. But a narrative speaks to our minds and emotions; it remains in our hearts. History is *His*-story. The Word of God is a narrative of existence—the greatest story ever told. Let us learn to communicate the character of God in stories that speak truth to the heart, like Jesus and the great storytelling kings.

Reflection Questions

1) Briefly summarize storytelling as seen in Scripture—what purposes did it serve?

2) Why was storytelling so important to Jesus' communication?

3) What is a "prophetic performer" and how can we encourage this gift among those in our communities?

Chapter 9

The Story to End All Stories

A small artist is content with art; a great artist is content with nothing except everything.

– G. K. Chesterton, Heretics

Creating with God

God's creativity is endless—every child, animal and sunrise display his infinite imagination. Throughout Scripture we see the meaning of his declaration, *"See, I am doing a new thing."*[82] Today the Spirit of God hovers over the darkness of the nations. He has chosen to work through us to bring light and life. We are created in God's image. His Holy Spirit, the same resurrection power which raised Christ from the dead, dwells in us. Will we demonstrate that power through the many forms of oral communication, ritual, ceremony, art, song, dance, drama, film and media? Are we going to celebrate God's diverse creativity in our cultures and be those who initiate new expressions of his beauty and glory?

It's easy to limit God to our own experiences. Indeed, often those most impacted by the last move of God are also those who most resist the next fresh thing he does. We become so comfortable with what first touched our hearts that we hold on to the patterns and symbols we associate with God's activity among us. But God is the Master Communicator who speaks to the hearts of every generation. His creative nature cannot be captured or put in a box—even the whole of creation cannot contain him or suspend his creativity. How can his creative communication flow through us, using all the tools he freely makes available to us in order to shape families, communities, and cultures?

"Through Us" is a short film set in the present day about how God shows himself in culture and creativity—through traditions, song and dance, and expressions of celebration. It is a call to action to use everything

---

82 Is 43:19 NIV

that we have been given and in all segments of society to play a part in communicating God's way. Watch here:

https://master-storyteller.net/films/through-us

Designing with the Spirit

Then the Lord said to Moses, 'See, I have chosen Bezalel son of Uri, the son of Hur, of the tribe of Judah, and I have filled him with the Spirit of God, with wisdom, with understanding, with knowledge and with all kinds of skills—to make artistic designs for work in gold, silver and bronze, to cut and set stones, to work in wood, and to engage in all kinds of crafts.'[83]

This passage from Exodus 31 comes after the Israelites had been freed from slavery, and were establishing recognizable and physical reminders of the Spirit of God that was present among them.

Bezalel is the first person in the Bible to be labeled "filled with the Holy Spirit"—the purpose of which was to create, design and "tell the story" by building the Tabernacle. The main reference to the Spirit of God in the Old Testament before this was in the creation story in Genesis chapter one when the Spirit of God was hovering over the waters and God said, "let there be light." As pointed out so eloquently:

The Spirit of God is intimately linked with the act of creation. So when we talk about Bezalel receiving the Spirit, we're really looking at the artistry of God as well. The act of Creation isn't described as the interplay of atoms and fundamental laws of physics; it's described in terms of art, architecture, creativity (look at Job 38, for instance, or Psalm 139). Further, when Ephesians 2:10 talks about us being God's "handiwork" it has connotations of us being God's works of art.[84]

83 Ex 31:1-5 NIV
84 Matt Hyde, "The Importance of Art: The Story of Bezalel (Exodus 31:1-10)," *MattsBibleBlog*, accessed August 28, 2017, https://mattsbibleblog.wordpress.com/2012/02/17/the-importance-of-art-the-story-of-bezalel-exodus-311-10/

ke the example of Bezalel as we are building the Kingdom of
g reminded to awaken to the Spirit and his creative purposes
in the ways we tell the story.

The Final Act: Revelation

What we refer to as the final "book" of the Bible is generally titled
Revelation or The Revelation of John. It begins with the words, *"The
revelation of Jesus Christ, which God gave unto him, to show to his servants
things which must shortly come to pass; and he sent and signified it by his angel
to his servant John. Who bare record of the word of God, and of the testimony
of Jesus Christ, and of all things that he saw."*[85] The record of the Revelation
itself begins several verses later with the words:

> *I was in the Spirit on the Lord's day, and heard behind me a
> great voice, as of a trumpet, saying, I am the Alpha and Omega,
> the first and the last: and, what you see write...and I turned to ·
> see the voice that spake with me. And being turned, I saw seven
> golden candlesticks; and in the midst of the seven candlesticks one
> like unto the Son of man...*[86]

Throughout the rest of the Revelation John describes what he *saw* and
heard. And what he saw and heard was practically beyond description.
There were dramatic scenes full of action that moved between time
frames and across vast geographies.

In the creation of films today we generally begin with a written script
which then goes through various stages of change, ultimately resulting in
a movie production. In the Revelation we have the opposite taking place.
What begins as an audio-visual show of epic proportions is reduced
to text in order to then be read to listeners. Revelation 1:3 says, *"Blessed
is the one who reads aloud the words of this prophecy, and blessed are those
who hear it and take to heart what is written in it."*[87] In John's time the only

---

85 Rv 1:1-2 KJV
86 Rv 1:10-13 KJV
87 Rv 1:3 NIV

technology available with which to record and transmit the Revelation was handwritten text, so it had to be written down and then read aloud to the people. It began as a multimedia oral communication, was converted to text, and then shared again in a single media oral form.

Movies, multi-media experiences, and even virtual reality are developing at faster and faster speeds. If these are things we are creating, what more has the Creator of the universe, who moves outside of our time and rhythms, already created that is beyond our imaginations? And could it be that the heavenly records which will be opened are not merely a book as we know it? But that all will see, hear and experience an otherworldly ultra-media presentation of the heavenly record of history, where not only the actions of mankind are revealed but his heart intent as well?

The Bible begins with a story of an enchanting garden and ends with an amazing and dramatic sci-fi-esque narrative. In between these bookends are riddles, proverbs, poems, songs, pictures, parables, letters and many more stories. In the book *Paul Faber, Surgeon*, George Macdonald writes,

> *God hides nothing. His very work from the beginning is revelation—a casting aside of veil after veil, a showing unto men of truth after truth. On and on, from fact to fact divine he advances, until at length in his Son Jesus he unveils his very face. Then begins a fresh unveiling, for the very work of the Father is the work the Son himself has to do—to reveal. His life was the unveiling of himself, and the unveiling of the Son is still going on, and is that for the sake of which the world exists. When he is unveiled, that is, when we know the Son, we shall know the Father also. The whole of creation, its growth, its history, the gathering total of human existence, is an unveiling of the Father. He is the life, the eternal life, the Only.*[88]

88 George MacDonald, *Paul Faber, Surgeon* (London: Hurst and Blackett, Publishers, 1879), Chapter 31.

The story is unfolding around us, being played out daily. We know the final act, but much of history is yet to be shaped through us. The story will not end until that final scene with every tribe, every nation, and every generation, welcoming Jesus and worshipping the Lamb, when our Creator says: *"It is done. I am the Alpha and the Omega, the Beginning and the End. To the thirsty I will give water without cost from the spring of the water of life."*[89]

Reflection Questions

1) How does the example of Bezalel highlight the way the Spirit of God leads us in creativity?

2) Have you ever considered yourself as having the ability or responsibility to create as empowered by the Holy Spirit?

3) Consider the many oral communication methods God has used to tell His story. What new applications of these principles can you apply in your setting?

   a. What would benefit your family?

   b. What could strengthen your church community?

   c. What might have wider cultural relevance and impact?

---

89 Rv 21:6 NIV

Epilogue

For Those Who Have Not Heard

GOD IS A communicating Father. He has used every means possible, both oral and textual, to give us his message of love and teach us his ways. Through his son we receive an inheritance and become his co-workers in the Great Storytelling Commission, inviting others to participate with us. The Revelation foretells the end of days when a great multitude of the redeemed from every nation, tribe and tongue will be gathered in worship before the throne of the living God.[90] Is it any wonder then that when the Holy Spirit was first poured out from heaven everyone heard the glories of God proclaimed in their own language?

Accomplishment of the Great Commission can be viewed as a supply chain. The end goal is to give every human being the opportunity to know God, to become a follower of Jesus. To achieve that goal every link in the supply chain must be functioning effectively. If any link is missing, or is weak, the entire outcome is jeopardized. Let's examine some of the critical steps essential to make it possible for every oral learner to become a follower of Jesus.

---

90 Rv 7:9-10

Still waiting for the story

Since you are reading this book you probably have access to a Bible in your own language. But what if you were part of the "oral majority" of the world, the over 60 percent who cannot, do not, or will not read? Or what if there were no orthography (writing system) for your language? How would you be able to engage with the Bible?

A man named Iskandar in Bihar, India had been afflicted with epilepsy. He would often go places and have a seizure which would cause him to fall and be unconscious and lost. He was told that if he went to the little village church he would be healed. He went to the pastor who prayed for him and gave him an audio Bible since he could not read. He listened to Scripture for four weeks and was healed of his epilepsy as he listened, and could then go about his business and even travel. Previously in 1955 his land was taken away and he and his family labored as slaves on the land. Now as a believer he prayed, "Lord you healed me; now help me get my land back." He then took the audio Bible to his landlord. After listening, the landlord could not sleep. He came to Iskandar and said "take the land back." The whole village heard about what had happened and they too came to faith in Jesus. Now Iskandar plays the audio Bible in front of his house with a speaker, and the village wants a church of their own.

Iskandar is one of over 104 million people living in 45,000 villages in Bihar. The average income is $1.25 per family per day. It is estimated by local church leaders that 80 percent of the population is functionally illiterate. There are six local languages, none of which have a full Bible.

Awareness of the need for orality-based methods of discipleship has increased in the Church. Orality has moved to the forefront of mission discussion and practice, and has begun to influence thought leaders and institutions. Since its inception, the International Orality Network (ION) has been influencing followers of Jesus around the globe to enable all oral learners to engage with the Word. In 2011, ION published a declaration on making disciples of the world's oral learners. This declaration states: "We believe that the foundation of discipleship is the shaping by, and obedience to, the word of God. It is the inalienable right and privilege of every person to have access to the word of God in his or her own heart language and in a media format he or she understands."[91]

If we hold this inalienable right to be true, then it is the obligation of followers of Jesus, those who have benefitted from having the Word of God, to provide access to those who do not yet have it. Nearly two thousand years have passed since Jesus walked this earth. Yet today, less than ten percent of the world's languages have a full Bible translation. As of the time of this publication fewer than 700 of the 7,097 languages of the world have a full Bible.[92] And though over 60 percent of the world are oral learners, fewer than 100 languages have a full audio Bible.[93] These figures highlight the nature of the unfinished task before us.

Further, Pew Foundation research indicates that unless people engage with the Word at least four times per week their core values and life practices do not change significantly.[94] Mission history among oral learners is rife with examples of the gospel being readily received—but since the people were unable to consistently engage with Scripture, their worldview remained unchanged. The end result was a syncretism in which Jesus was added to the pre-existing array of gods and values, and did not radically change their core belief system.

Lessons from missions history underscore the critical importance of enabling every oral learner to be able to engage with God's Word in a media format they understand. We know that in order to believe, people must first hear and understand the message of the Gospel. However, we

91 "ION Declaration on Making Disciples of Oral Learners," *International Orality Network*, 2011, accessed August 28, 2017, https://orality.net/declaration/.

92 "2016 Annual Report," *4.2.20 Foundation*, 2017, accessed August 29, 2017, https://4220foundation.com/masters/4.2.20-Foundation-Annual-Report-2016.pdf.

93 "God Speaks. Can They Listen?" *Davar Partners*, accessed August 30, 2017, https://www.davarpartners.com/Main/Page/1.

94 Allison Pond, Scott Clement and Gregory Smith, "Religion Among the Millennials" *Pew Forum on Religion and Public Life*, 2010, accessed August 16, 2017, http://www.pewforum.org/2010/02/17/religion-among-the-millennials/.

must also understand that in order for them to grow in faith they need access to the whole Word of God in their own language and in a format they understand. This access is often one of the missing links. As in the story of Iskandar in Bihar, the Bible has not been translated into the languages of the local people. And even if it was, the people could not engage with it because they do not read.

Every one of us has a greater or lesser reliance upon orality or textuality as our mode of communication. The Orality Index[95] indicates the degree of one's orality reliance along an orality-textuality continuum. Those who have become overly text-reliant can sometimes miss so much of God's communication because they have narrowed the channels through which they receive and process communication. Oral communicators, however, learn to hone their listening and observational skills, and therefore frequently have far more developed memories than people who depend upon text as a primary information storage repository. So orality is not a fad but rather pertains to the very essence of human communication—how we receive, process, remember and transmit information.

Importance of the Old Testament

"If it was good enough for Paul it is good enough for me." This tongue-in-cheek phrase is sometimes heard in the context of debates over Bible translations. What we often don't stop to think about is that the Bible used by Jesus, the disciples and Paul was the Old Testament. All parts of Scripture are important in giving the full revelation of the mystery of the Word of God, the Davar.

As invaluable as the New Testament is, it nonetheless cannot stand alone. As a Filipino church leader said, "The New Testament without the Old Testament is like a machete without a handle." Knowledge of the Old Testament and its language is essential to understanding the New Testament. It prepares the way for comprehension of our need of

---

95 An instrument for assessing orality reliance developed by a team of specialists as part of an on-going orality mapping project of the Center for Oral Scriptures. www.centerfororalscriptures.com.

a Messiah, his atoning sacrifice, and the coming of the Kingdom of God. God sent his son "in the fullness of time"[96]—in God's masterplan he strategically chose not to send the Savior until he had first given Israel the Tanakh or Old Testament. It is the foundation upon which the New Testament builds.

From start to finish the New Testament contains quotations, paraphrases and references to the Old Testament. The New Testament quotes 61 of the 66 books of the Old Testament. Roger Nicole states that on average 1 in 22.5 verses of the New Testament is a quotation of the Old Testament. If all references and clear allusions are considered, over 10 percent of the New Testament consists of citations from the Old Testament.[97]

The Old Testament addresses God's authority over every sphere of life and society. Besides this, the Old Testament is important to oral cultures due to characteristics which many of them share with the people of the Old Testament. Many oral cultures identify closely with the stories and the community norms and practices of Israel in the Hebrew Bible (Old Testament). The Old Testament is, after all, a textual record of God's communication with an oral people group. Samuel Chiang has stated, "No church planting movement has been sustained long term without access to the whole Bible."[98] It is no wonder that God planned for 74% of the Bible to be the Old Testament.

Despite the incredible value of the Old Testament, we too often dismiss its importance in the process of evangelism. We see the salvation story as centered on the Gospels, and forget the context of the whole story, which started at the beginning of time and has never stopped. God does not dip in and out of history. He never ceased speaking, nor is he silent today. When people can't or prefer not to read, he can still speak to them. When people don't understand a message because it isn't

---

96 Gal 4:4
97 Roger Nicole, *Revelation and the Bible*, ed. Carl. F.H. Henry (Grand Rapids: Baker, 1958) 137-151.
98 David Swarr, "Advancing Scripture Access for Discipleship Among Bible-less Oral People" *MissionFrontiers.org*, 2014, accessed August 28, 2017, http://www.missionfrontiers.org/issue/article/advancing-scripture-access-for-discipleship-among-bible-less-oral-people.

being communicated to their whole being, God is still the greatest storyteller. We are the ones who limit him to textual communication and teaching methods through our narrow view of what is possible.

Vital translation

But what about communities that do not have the whole Bible in their own language? How does the local Body of Christ disciple its children without the Old Testament stories of Joseph, David, Esther and Daniel? How does the community learn God's standards of righteousness, justice, or governance without the Old Testament? The completion of the Great Commission depends upon the translation of the full Bible into the languages of these people groups.

Efforts are being made by translation agencies to accelerate the process of translation, but there are a number of bottlenecks which impede the progress, particularly in translation of the Old Testament. One is that there are too few translators proficient[99] in biblical Hebrew. A second is the lack of sufficient next-generation translators and consultants in the workforce. Third is that there are few translation training models which are attractive and appropriate for the emerging generation. Each of these three bottlenecks is an essential link in the supply chain and must be addressed in order for the overall goal to be achieved.

The ideal way to learn a language is by immersion in the language itself; this is how each of us has learned our mother tongue. The best way to become proficient in Arabic or Chinese, or any language, is to be immersed in that environment and culture, constantly hearing and being forced to speak in the language. But this has not been the case in traditional approaches to teaching biblical Hebrew for the simple reason that until the second half of the last century there was nowhere for the Christian community to send someone for immersion in the language. Therefore, the only possible approach to learning biblical Hebrew has been a "grammar-translation" approach. While this has merit it also has

---

99 By "proficient" we mean able to function within the language as independent translators/ consultants according to standards that would be acceptable for official documentation.

some deficiencies in that it is not the most "natural" approach to learning a language and has the unintended effects of creating hurdles and narrowing the gate to those who might otherwise learn biblical Hebrew.

The Bible tells us that God does things "in the fullness of time."[100] At the very time that he is moving the Body of Christ to accelerate translation of the Word of God—including the Old Testament—into all languages, he has provided a means for immersion in biblical Hebrew. Translators in training can now be immersed in Hebrew in Israel. It is now possible to learn Hebrew in Hebrew. This means that even someone from a far off tribe in a remote area of the world can learn to translate the Old Testament directly into their own language without needing to work through a third language or world view. This method can also improve the quality of translation, accelerate the process, and cut down on the costs.

Designing for everyone

The value of learning the deeper meanings of God's communication through the process of learning Hebrew goes beyond just translation. God's Word provides the essential content and then gives us the freedom to determine how best to contextualize and express that content in a meaningful way. At any point in our personal or corporate history, and in every cultural setting, we have the privilege and responsibility to conduct our practices in ways that enable the essential to remain. For indeed, *"The grass withers and the flowers fall, but the word of our God endures forever."*[101]

God has deposited treasures that reflect his glory in every culture. These treasures are waiting to be found, celebrated and invested to bring redemptive transformation. Some are right on the surface ready for use. Others may be buried because sin and misuse have covered the cultural terrain. Reclaiming the value of a cultural heritage may require taking back stolen goods that have accumulated destructive associations, by intentionally reinterpreting their meanings and cleansing the

---

100 Gal 4:4
101 Isaiah 40:8 NIV

associations. Whatever the case may be in your context, the treasures are there and can be found by those with pure hearts who will ask, seek and knock.

Further, as we think of outreach and discipleship of oral communities, it is important to keep every segment of society in mind, and to devise strategies which are appropriate and tailored for each. The Lord was very clear in his instruction to Israel that everyone in the community was to engage with his Word: men, women, children, even the aliens in their midst. The same is true for us today. There are many demographic categories and segments into which communities are divided. Each context and community is also unique. The important thing is to carefully examine the natural affinities within the community, to determine the degree of oral reliance of each, and then to devise methods and tools appropriate to each.

Our Creator is the Master Storyteller. His creativity in communication is unparalleled. He has demonstrated for us oral strategies to instruct entire communities and even a nation; he has modeled for us a multiplicity of methodologies of oral communication; and he has given us a commission to go and do likewise, along with the promise that he will be with us in every circumstance and situation. We are called to believe in the now invisible, so as to create with God, joining the Master Storyteller in the completion of His-story.

MASTER
STORYTELLER

DIGITAL LEARNING COMMUNITY

EVERY PURCHASE OF MASTER STORYTELLER GIVES ACCESS
TO AN INTERACTIVE LEARNING PLATFORM.

READ THE BOOK & WATCH THE FILMS ONLINE

EXCLUSIVE AUDIO, VISUAL ART, AND RELATED LINKS &
RESOURCES - *ADDED REGULARLY*

CONTRIBUTE STORIES & NEW MEDIA

DISCOVER & GROW TOGETHER WITH A GLOBAL COMMUNITY
OF LEARNERS

DIGITAL.MASTER-STORYTELLER.NET

MASTER
STORYTELLER

SWARR GIDOOMAL ARAUJO

DAVID SWARR PHD.
Executive Director,
International Orality
Network
President/CEO, 4.2.20
Foundation

RICKI GIDOOMAL
Chief of Staff, 4.2.20
Foundation
Senior Associate,
Communications,
International Orality
Network

PSALM ARAUJO
Creative Director,
Communications &
Special Projects, 4.2.20
Foundation

Master Storyteller is a project of the Center for Oral Scriptures (COS)–a program of the 4.2.20 Foundation committed to advancing access and engagement with the whole Word of God for every language, culture, and people. The team of three who created this project share extensive exposure to the land of the Bible and to Hebrew language and tradition. Together they also created the short film trilogy produced in Israel.

All proceeds from this book and production go toward the work of the Center for Oral Scriptures in serving oral learners.

Made in the USA
Coppell, TX
16 August 2021